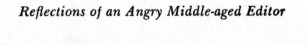

Reflections of an Angry Middle-aged Editor

REFLECTIONS

OF AN

ANGRY

MIDDLE-AGED

EDITOR

by James A. Wechsler

Essay Index Reprint Series

BOOKS FOR LIBRARIES PRESS
FREEPORT, NEW YORK

Library of Congress Cataloging in Publication Data
Freeport, N.Y., Books
Wechsler, James Arthur, 1915- for Libraries Press
    Reflections of an angry middle-aged editor. [1971, c1960]
245p (Essay index reprint series)
    1. U. S.--Politics and government--1953-1961.
2. Public opinion--U. S. I. Title. (Series)
E835.W4 1971   973.921   72-37152
ISBN 0-8369-2524-6

PRINTED IN THE UNITED STATES OF AMERICA
BY
NEW WORLD BOOK MANUFACTURING CO., INC.
HALLANDALE, FLORIDA 33009

To Michael and Holly

Author's Note

I AM INDEBTED to a number of people for generous advice and assistance in the preparation of this book. Some of them are in general agreement with the views expressed; some differ sharply with me at varied points; some were consulted primarily about specific sections. But I do want to thank all of them for their help, while, of course, reserving to myself total responsibility for what is said. Those who have helped me follow:

Benjamin V. Cohen, Alvin Davis, Theodore Kaghan, Norman Kelman, Max Lerner, William T. McCleery, Ted Poston, Joseph L. Rauh, Jr., Irwin Ross, Dorothy Schiff, Arthur Schlesinger, Jr., William V. Shannon, Herbert Wechsler.

I value the friendship of all of them, and trust this volume inflicted undue pain on none.

Cecile M. Eddy provided invaluable editorial and technical help in preparing the manuscript and I am, as always, indebted to Nancy Wechsler for wise, patient and fearless comment.

James A. Wechsler
NEW YORK, FEBRUARY 10, 1960

Contents

PART I

THE BLAND AND

THE BEAT

CHAPTER 1

The Age of Unthink

TWO SEPARATE episodes inspired the reflections that led to the writing of this book, and perhaps it is appropriate to begin by recalling them.

On the evening of November 6, 1958, I took part in a symposium on the Beat Generation at Hunter College. The event, if it may be so described, was sponsored by Brandeis University; the other participants were Jack Kerouac, author of *On the Road* and self-proclaimed voice of the Beat Generation; Kingsley Amis, the talented, witty British writer who admits to being neither young nor angry but has been so labeled on two continents; and Professor Ashley Montagu, the noted anthropologist.

I almost missed the meeting, proving that books, like other productions, are prey to the accident of history. It occurred just two days after the state elections of that year; I was still tired, if not beat, and the prospect of a long evening of recitation and listening seemed less congenial than, say, watching a basketball game at Madison Square Garden.

But I had a certain curiosity about Kerouac, whom I had never seen, and about the subject, which I had heard discussed with increasing frequency and earnestness by my son (then sixteen) and some of his friends. In fact I had begun to feel out of touch. So, though ill-prepared to deliver a speech (and even less prepared for what happened), I reached the auditorium a few moments after Kerouac had begun what turned out to be a forty-minute rendition, and there was more than one reprise.

My first astonishment was the size of the audience. As one apparently addicted to public speech since an early age, I have grown accustomed to addressing empty seats as well as uplifted drowsy countenances. I had steeled myself for the sight of unoccupied leather. Instead, on arrival at the entrance, I discovered that this was what is known in the trade as an SRO affair, with scores of young people milling around outside the auditorium in the vain hope that the capacity of the hall would be expanded by the rhetoric inside.

Having forgotten there was a stage entrance, I proceeded at once to the main door where a strong-minded young woman effectively barred the way. The meeting had begun and I tried perhaps impatiently to tell her I was one of the scheduled performers; at first this evoked almost no reaction except massive resistance. I could not tell whether she thought I was an impostor or whether she had been intimidated by the Fire Department; anyway, after producing my press card and adopting a tone of entreaty rather than insistence, I was finally admitted.

As I walked a trifle uncomfortably down the center aisle to the stage, I got my first view of the leader of the Beat Generation. He was attired in a lumberjack shirt unadorned by tie, but there was nothing especially ostentatious about his lack of dress. A little more flabbergasting was the discovery that he was holding what proved to be a glass of brandy, and throughout the evening he made several trips to the wings for a refill. Kerouac acknowledged my arrival by observing, "You ruined my sentence," and then resumed a discourse which I am obliged to describe as a stream of semiconsciousness.

The audience was predominantly, if not exclusively, young —ranging from high-school students to college seniors, and with a sprinkling of the middle-aged and the old. With due reverence for Messrs. Amis, Montagu and myself, a large proportion of those present had obviously come to see and hear Kerouac, which, after all, explained my own belated presence too. There was plainly a bloc of the committed beat reveling in each of his mischievous irrelevancies and with whom he used a kind of sign language mystifying to outsiders; there were also what might be called the fellow travelers of the beat, some of whom manifested bewilderment and even impatience with the Leader by the time the evening had ended. There were, also, no doubt some who had just come for the show.

I cannot recall as large an assemblage of young people— except for the captive audiences of school assemblies—since the radical heyday of the thirties. The beat, of course, do not carry membership cards and one has no way of knowing how many true disciples were recruited or disaffected by Kerouac's chaotic exhibition. But the size of the turnout was extraordinary.

Having listened to a recording of the evening's proceedings and pondered a transcript, I still find myself largely out of Kerouac's reach. I am, admittedly, eight years older than he—forty-three to his thirty-five the night of the symposium at Hunter—but such a gap is not normally considered prohibitive among adults. I was on speaking terms with a lot of men some years younger than Kerouac. Moreover I brought no instinctive hostility to the occasion (toward the end, in one of his most coherent thrusts, he cried, "You came here prepared to attack me," but in fact I had come, as previously indicated, utterly unprepared, period).

There were times when he sounded like a jaded traveling salesman telling obscene bedtime stories to the young; there were others when the melancholy of his cadences achieved a mildly hypnotic effect, so that one listened to it as if hearing an obscure but appealing fragment of music. There were also many intervals that can only be described as gibberish. Thus at one point he was chanting (and I quote from the transcript):

In fact here is a poem I've written about Harpo Marx:

> Harpo, I'll always love you.
> Oh Harpo, when did you seem like an angel the
>   last and played the gray harp of gold?
> When did you steal the silverware and buckspray
>   the guests?
> When did your brother find rain in your sunny
>   courtyard?
> When did you chase your last blond across a
>   millionaire's lawn with a bait hook on a
>   line protruding from your bicycle?
> Oh, when last you powderpuffed your white flower
>   face with a fish barrel cover?
> Harpo, who is that lion I saw you with? . . .

Without questioning the place of Harpo Marxism in history, I find little rhyme or reason in these observations, and the Leader drooped to the dimensions of ham. The totality of his performance, brightened as it was by flashes of imagery, was a union of madness and sadness; by the end the occasional vivid or moving phrase seemed like an isolated line of poetry surrounded by vulgar ramblings on a latrine wall.

Kerouac is dark-haired and sturdily built (he played football for a year for Lou Little at Columbia and, when he quit,
the coach said prophetically that the "boy was tired"). He
has rather graceful gestures; he alternates murmurs of furtive sexuality with intimations of high piety. He deftly evokes
the emotional loyalty of those who feel that they too are
beat. It is no irreverence, I trust, to say that at moments he
might have been called the Billy Gloomy-Sunday of our time.

Did we ever establish any communication? I think we
did; at least there is no other way I can explain the furious
feeling he exhibited in the exchange that took place after
the allegedly prepared recitals had occurred.

KEROUAC: . . . James Wechsler. Who's James Wechsler?
Right over there. James Wechsler, you believe in the destruction of America, don't you?

WECHSLER: No. (The transcript added "laughter.")

KEROUAC: What do you believe in, come here, come here
and tell me what you believe in . . . You told me what you
don't believe in. I want to know what you do believe in.
(Cries from the audience: "That's right.") This is a university, we've got to learn . . . I believe in love, I vote for
love (applause).

It was rather difficult to avoid a pretentious reply:

WECHSLER: I believe in the capacity of the human intelligence to create a world in which there is love, compassion,
justice and freedom. I believe in fighting for that kind of
world. I think what you are doing is to try to destroy anybody's instinct to care about this world.

KEROUAC: I believe, I believe in the dove of peace.

WECHSLER: So do I.

KEROUAC: No you don't. You're fighting with me for the
dove of peace. You came here prepared to attack me.

It went on for a little while longer and then the chairman mercifully explained that it was very late, and in truth it was a few minutes after ten.

There is no point in indefinitely prolonging the reportorial agony. This was hardly a debate in which anyone could have scored the points; I was grappling with a man in outer space, and it was only for the briefest of intervals that we even seemed to occupy the same mat. I shall never quite understand why he assumed I had come there with a plot, or even why he responded so angrily to a minor quip I made at President Eisenhower's expense, this being a time when even Republican newspapers were ceasing to regard Eisenhower as above criticism.

Kerouac had observed, if that is the proper term:

Well, Mr. Wechsler, I was sitting under a tangerine tree in Florida one afternoon and I was trying to translate the Diamond Sutra from Sanskrit to English and I said shall I call it a personal god or an impersonal god, and at that moment a little tangerine dropped out of the tree and they only drop out of a tree about once every six weeks and landed right square in the middle of my head. Right, boing; I said, okay, personal god.

Somewhat testily I interjected:

I just want to say, Mr. Kerouac, that as an editor I have to write about Dwight D. Eisenhower's press conference every week—

KEROUAC (interrupting): He's very witty—

WECHSLER:—and it's possible to reduce life to an area of so little sense that there would hardly be any reason for all these people to have come here tonight, or for us to be here. I don't think we render any service by doing that—

KEROUAC: Education is education.

WECHSLER: Well, as Eisenhower would say government is government.

KEROUAC: And as Dulles would say, statesmanship is statesmanship.

For that small moment we seemed like two quarreling editorial writers occupying the same planet.

Dr. Joseph Kauffman, the soft-voiced moderator, gently interpolated that "the point which Mr. Wechsler makes is one which is fairly commonly held among people who are considered activists in the sense of social and political action."

In what I must characterize as a growl Kerouac responded: "Don't give me that stuff. I'm going out of this atmosphere."

In a sense, that is the last I saw of him.

What I had tried to say was embodied in an earlier statement that evening; since it is rather awkwardly relevant to the conception of this book, perhaps some words of it should be published here:

"It is a strange thing to participate in this symposium because I guess that I am one of the few unreconstructed radicals of my generation, and much of what has happened in the last twenty and twenty-five years has challenged many of the things that I believe in deeply. Yet my basic sense about what I care about in the world, what I fight for, what I believe in is remarkably unaltered.

"I have to say to you that, with due respect to Mr. Kerouac, I see no really major point in this kind of organized confusionism . . . To me the astonishing thing, after all these years of our time and our century which have been brutal, cruel and difficult years, is that we can still find, if I may say so, a Boris Pasternak, and he is only a name and a symbol;

but that all over the world there does seem to be a sense of the survival of human values and decency which seem to me to be the only things that give meaning to life . . .

"The impressive fact is that there survives and that there recurs and is renewed among young kids all over the world the sense that there are values of decency worth fighting for and even giving one's life for.

"There was a man named Felix Cohen who died when he was forty-six. He was the son of Morris Raphael Cohen and he wrote a great essay which has meant a great deal to me in my life in which he argued that the astonishing thing about our world is that, given all the travail and the turmoil and the sadness, it does seem to be true that certain ethical values do re-emerge and that children grow up sensing them and understanding them.

"I do not happen to be a religious man in any conventional sense but I do have the sense that what gives meaning to life is the survival of these values. And so it is that there are people all the time all over the world who, when they see cruelty and injustice and intolerance and bigotry often risk many things to fight against these incredible conditions. Now I know there is a view that this is probably because they were dropped on their heads when they were small children. But I thought Arthur Koestler answered that point rather well when he said that, if we really believed that the only people who have any decent instincts in the world are those who were dropped on their heads when they were babies, it's very hard to make any sense out of life . . .

"I think there are values that have transcended these difficult and complicated conditions of human existence. It is a sad thing about America now that what is regarded as the great revolt and the great representation of dissent and unorthodoxy is what is called the beat generation. Because I guess it has very little meaning to me and, after listening to its spokesman tonight, I must say that I find myself groping in the darkest confusion as to what the hell this is about (from audience: "Shame on you"). (Laughter and applause.) There is the right, thank God, for all of us to scream and shout and do anything we damn please in public. There is also, I think, the responsibility for us to try to give to the people in our society some sense of what matters and what is important and what we care about.

"People say so often that there are no issues any longer, that everything was settled by the New Deal and the Fair Deal, and that there really aren't any great differences in political life. To some extent that's true. Yet we live in a time when there are two things that seem to me to be worthy of everything within us.

"One is the fact that there is something called the hydrogen bomb which can make a mockery of anything we call civilization. The other is the quest for human equality which has become the dominant and decisive issue of our lifetime in America. So it never has seemed to me really that there is nothing left to fight for, or that there is nothing worth arguing about in our society."

There were far better words spoken that evening by both Dr. Amis and Professor Montagu than any recited by Kerouac or myself.

Dr. Amis suggested amiably but pointedly that there was no genuine union between the so-called angry young men of Great Britain, who had at least voiced a certain definable—and not monolithic—protest against the grayness of life, and the rambling wrecks from American Tech who had ostentatiously proclaimed themselves the beat generation.

Professor Montagu, perhaps because he had not been accused of being angry, perhaps because an anthropologist acquires a certain occupational patience with the eccentricities of man, spoke with the greatest compassion: "What I am trying to say is that it is not condemnation or contempt that is called for but compassion and understanding, that the beat generation is not something either to bemoan or disown but a suffering confusion of human beings crying out for sympathetic understanding. The beat generation represents the ultimate expression of a civilization whose moral values have broken down and in many ways, what is even worse, a civilization with little faith or conviction in the values it professes to believe. (From audience—"Right!")

"Its ideal values are one thing. But its real values—the values by which it lives—are quite another. Our ideal and our real values are in conflict. The Sermon on the Mount and the principle of competition are simply not compatible with one another. And this fact gives rise to the great hypocrisy of a society that preaches the one and lives by the other, and it gives rise, among other things, to a demoralization of the sort which results in beatniks.

"Human beings living in a society in which such mutually irreconcilable, such conflicting and false values are dominant are likely to be confused and confusing. Those who subscribe to such values damage not only themselves but wreak havoc upon their children, many of whom constitute members of the beat generation.

"The beatniks know that there is too much that is wrong with the non-beatniks, but they are thoroughly confused as to why it is that what is wrong is wrong. Their cult of unthink is of no help, nor is resort to esoteric cults and Eastern religion.

"Whatever it is they're in revolt against we must take care that the anarchy that is so apparent in the beat generation is not mistaken for anything other than it is, namely a signal of distress, a cry for love, a refusal to accept defeat at the hands of the unloving lovers who made them what they are.

"We owe a debt of gratitude to the beat writers for so forcefully articulating what the less vocal members of this generation feel and think."

In the anarchy of the evening these were the most generous and thoughtful phrases, and they were plainly addressed to an audience beyond the gathering of the moment. They created a stillness and reserve that had been lacking throughout the previous recitations, as if even the most frenetic Kerouacians had been persuaded for the instant to think of themselves in a larger context. But I suppose there were also those who whispered to themselves and their neighbors that Professor Montagu was an amiable square who just wasn't getting enough kicks.

At the end there was the usual flurry around the platform and I did not get a chance to talk to Kerouac again. We probably would not have had much to say to each other. I felt both very young and very old: young, in the sense that it seemed to me I found life less overwhelming than Kerouac did, and old because I knew I could not offer any simplicities comparable to his platform of raucous hedonism.

At the start I noted there were two incidents which quite coincidentally provoked this book. One was the Kerouac affair; the other was a small gathering in a suite at the Hotel Commodore in New York just a few weeks later.

This was an informal session arranged by Joseph L. Rauh Jr., who had for some eleven years been the solid pillar of an organization known as Americans for Democratic Action, an enterprise perhaps more celebrated for the attacks leveled against it in the conservative press than for any political revolutions it has truly engineered. Rauh was what Heywood Broun must have had in mind when he referred to the species "congenital liberal"; a large, warm, forceful and resourceful man who was probably more responsible than any other individual for the sustained existence of those formidable initials ADA, not to be confused with the American Dental Association.

The subject of the gathering might have been summed up quite simply as: where do we go from here, or, what are we up to, anyway? After more than a decade of life ADA was accepted in right-wing political circles as a major menace and regarded with almost equal anxiety by many liberal politicians who feared someone would remember they had once been associated with it. Certain views as to the circumstances which produced this unhappy state of the organization will be examined later, as well as some of the self-appraisals advanced at this assemblage.

In the aftermath of the Kerouac episode what struck me most as we met was that the youngest man in this room was Arthur Schlesinger, Jr., who had just passed his fortieth birthday.

The roll call of those present is less important than the knowledge that there was not among us a single person representing the generation born between 1925 and 1935. Possibly this discovery was especially poignant for those of us who had once been identified as leaders of "the youth movement." Yet perhaps it also underlined an even more striking American occurrence, which is that those of us who had the good or bad fortune to become twenty in the 1930's have been granted a certain immortality by the nonemergence of younger voices. In an essay in *The New Leader*'s symposium on the Young Generation, Dan Bell put the matter quite entertainingly.

Having joined the Young People's Socialist League in 1932 at the advanced age of thirteen, he noted, and graduated from CCNY in 1938, he found himself being described nearly twenty years later as a "young sociologist." Pitilessly documenting the point that we were in that strange condition where life seemed to begin at forty, he added:

Some years ago Harvey Swados, then about 38, published an exciting first novel and was called a promising "young" writer; Richard Hofstadter who, at the age of 42, has published four or five first-rate historical interpretations, is called a young American scholar; James Wechsler, over 40, a young editor; Saul Bellow, over 40, a young American novelist; Alfred Kazin, 41, a young American critic, etc.

All that was published in April, 1957, and we youths are now that much older. We have even been called "grouchy middle-aged men," but by and large we retain a kind of immunity from underage attack if only because we manage to make more tumultuous sounds than those born ten or twenty years later.

Time plays harsh tricks. Even as I write this I am conscious that some who will read it do not know what it meant to be on this earth during the Spanish Civil War, when at last there was an international brigade composed of men prepared to risk their lives for the salvation of mankind, and for no private or provincial cause. A young man of twenty-five was four when all that occurred, as I was four when the Treaty of Versailles was signed.

To establish any continuity is hard enough. Yet I venture to say that as a youth of twenty I felt no large gap between myself and those who—when I was twelve—had been engaged in the effort to save the lives of two unheralded human beings named Sacco and Vanzetti. As I grew up their lost cause had become mine, and I felt no difficulty about comprehending the depth of feeling my elders associated with it.

The beatnik proclaims his alienation and his irresponsibility, and his contempt for those who have the effrontery to seek to influence the affairs of men or establish order in the gone universe. But no single voice really speaks for him. Kerouac at Hunter was a caricature of the breed; on another evening in a different setting at Columbia, Allen Ginsberg, (whom Kerouac had dragged onto the stage like a circus donkey the night of our meeting) recited poetry in a fashion that Diana Trilling found extraordinarily moving and intelligible, and led her to feel pity rather than disdain for him and his cohorts. She added: "Whatever one's view of the poetry, the manners, the compulsive disreputableness and the sometimes ostentatious homosexuality of those who term themselves beat, it is perhaps most noteworthy that their form of protest is almost wholly nonpolitical, and at moments a rebellion against politics itself."*

The ranks of the beat are limited and scattered. It is hardly likely that what they are up to would evoke so much notice if most of their contemporaries were engaged in great exercises; what gives them part of their prominence—as it did "the lost" of the 1920's and the radicals of the 1930's—is that they almost alone seem to care very deeply, even if it is about the cult of not caring. If their escapades are tinged with exhibitionism and even vulgarity, they create a certain fascination because they at least seem to be crazily alive while so many others are just going through the motions. Their commitment to disaffection is intense.

Perhaps they interest us, too, because politics seems to have become less and less relevant to many of the young

* See *Partisan Review*, Spring, 1959.

people growing up in the land, and among the beat the estrangement is most fully burlesqued.

We have never had political youth movements comparable to those of Europe and Latin America. Some three decades ago Harold Laski was asking "Why Don't Your Young Men Care?" and even in the turbulent 1930's the number of activists in Communist and Socialist enterprises, not to speak of the major parties, was far smaller than it has often appeared in retrospect (although their experiences touched a wider fragment of their generation than may have been realized at the time). In any case what we are now encountering is large-scale disassociation. Many young men and women who enter politics do so with a view to their own political careers, rather than out of any tenacious conviction; the local reform movements of today too frequently become the entrenched bureaucracies of tomorrow.

This book does not presume to offer any definitive judgment about the beat. Rather, as indicated at the start, they are the catalyst for some random discussion of the state of "beatness" amid which most of the politics of the day is conducted, of the failures of political leaders to impart any quality of excitement and élan to their endeavors; and for an affirmation and elaboration of certain positions which, I trust, form some basis for a political revival.

It is not the kids with beards and blue jeans, "many of them publicly homosexual, talking about or taking drugs, assuring us they are out of their minds, not responsible," in Mrs. Trilling's words, about whom this is primarily written. Rather it is about the young fogies, the minor Machiavellis, the gray-flanneled status seekers, the modern Republicans and the "realistic" Democrats, the tired liberals and ex-Communists turned raucous patrioteers, and the "men of moderation" in whose hands great issues have become great bores. Possibly this look at things will parenthetically explain what the rest of us look like to the beat and why it is they seem so self-righteously convinced that it is their elders who are the sad specimens.

CHAPTER 2

Is Everybody Happy?

ONE MAY advance a variety of diagnoses for the malaise that afflicts the politics of our time, alternately driving young men and women into the comfortable refuges of suburbia and the beatnik joints of San Francisco. At first glance they seem to add up to the conflicting propositions that things are too good and too bad, too simple and too complex, too bright and too dark.

The view most commonly advanced by Henry Luce's publications is that America is so giddy a success story that it has rendered militant political liberalism obsolete. The poor, we are told, are virtually no longer with us; the rich have learned to accommodate themselves to the realities of the welfare state; the middle class is serenely clipping its coupons, and the workman is driving his Chrysler. In this opulent land the New Dealer, the Fair Dealer, the Square Dealer, or whatever name one chooses to describe the man, is a rebel without a cause. If certain inequities persist in human relations, if there remain "pockets of discontent," they are being steadily overcome by "moderate" measures; if the threat of annihilation hangs over the world, that is being met with resolution and fortitude by hard-headed Republican man-

agers of our destinies, in co-operation with Democratic statesmen like Majority Leader Lyndon Johnson who are never
to be confused with "left-wing Democrats" and other screw-
balls. Admittedly the garbage man's life is still a smelly one,
but it is infinitely worse in Russia. For America and Britain
alike, cried *Life* not long ago, "the abundant life is already
a fact."

When the President embarked for Europe in August, 1959,
Time affirmed that "the U.S. that Dwight D. Eisenhower
left behind him that week was one in which fear and fretting
were made ridiculous by the facts of national life." (In the
same week, *Newsweek, Time*'s competitor, reported that 58
percent of American college students had chosen *Mad* as
their favorite magazine.)

That is *Time*'s American cover story, and it has sold well.
It has permeated the political world, coloring the attitudes
and guiding the strategies of ambitious men. The portrait
may be intermittently marred by the harassment of Negro
school children in Little Rock, by recession in Detroit, by
a slum fire in New York, by school shortage in Chicago, by
the discovery of an unexpectedly high level of fallout in St.
Louis' milk, by even some flash of revelation about the lone-
liness and emptiness of both a highly paid executive or
industrial worker's existence. These are the random disturbances of democracy; they do not alter the majesty of the
portrait. America, we are told, is busy, America is prosperous, America is preoccupied with the reaping of its golden
harvest, and America looks only for leaders who will sustain
the general glow. Let the hell raisers face it; they are out
of date.

Obviously there are elements of validity in this idyll. It
is a truer estimate of the American condition than the one
which *Pravda* and *Izvestia* normally give their readers. That

there are large flaws and self-deceptions in it will be contended later; but *Time's* view of the nation is important if
only because it is accepted by so much of the press and by
so many political figures who are swayed by what they read
or what is read to them.

Much of the same thing has been said by others, and some
of those saying it most vociferously were once the angriest
critics of the American scene. The "rediscovery of America"
became a fashionable pursuit among intellectuals in the
1950's. For many this was expiation for the folly of their
romance with Soviet Communism; having finally recognized
the nature of the beast, they could feel only uncritical passion for the girl they had left behind.

Thus the image of "settling down" ceased to portend a
life of drab accommodation; it became an act of positive
virtue and maturity. In a symposium on the Younger Generation published by *The New Leader*, Norman Podhoretz
saluted the new era as a time when young people learned
that "the real adventure of existence was to be found not
in radical politics or in Bohemia but in the 'moral life' of
the individual, within the framework of his efforts to do his
duty and assume his responsibilities in a world of adults.

"The mistake of the thirties had been to suppose that
society could ever be more than a bad bargain with the
absolute; to the younger generation American society seemed
on the whole a reasonably decent environment for the intellectual . . . they discovered that 'conformity' did not necessarily mean dullness and unthinking conventionality, that,
indeed, there was great beauty, profound significance in a
man's struggle to achieve freedom *through* submission to
conditions . . . The trick, then, was to stop carping at life
like a petulant adolescent . . . and to get down to the business of adult living as quickly as possible. And get down to

business the young generation did. A great many of them married early; most of them made firm and decisive commitments to careers of a fairly modest kind, such as teaching; they cultivated an interest in food, clothes, furniture, manners—these being elements of the 'richness' of life that the generation of the thirties had deprived itself of. As befitted responsible adults, there was nothing playful or frisky about these young people . . . Very much aware of how complicated and difficult all problems were, very much alive to the dangers of ideologies and enthusiasms and passions, very much persuaded that *la verité reste dans les nuances,* they struck a perfect attitude of the civilized adult: poised, sober, judicious, prudent."

Granted that there remained the fact of the atomic bomb, and the nervousness it might induce; admittedly "one was living in a world of severely limited possibilities, balanced precariously on the edge of an apocalypse." The truth was that "in such a world there was very little one could know, very little one could do." So one buckled down to the intriguing duties and diversions of existence, presumably leaving the bomb for the adolescents and the aged to worry about.

While Podhoretz expressed concern about the problem of "unearned maturity—a maturity that has become a means of protecting one's neat little existence from the disruptive incursions of experience," he felt obliged to add the dubious defense that "the prime virtue of a period of cold war and atomic stalemate must necessarily be prudence."

Reading this ode to a "non-generation," it was difficult to avoid thinking of the editor of the magazine in which it appeared—a warm, zestful, sixty-five-year-old immigrant named Sol Levitas, who has devoted most of his life to warring against oppression, injustice and all varieties of man's inhumanities to man, and who never seems to have suffered from combat fatigue; one wondered whether things have gone so awry that the young have suddenly grown old, while the old, refusing to fade away, momentarily halt the clock.

Podhoretz, of course, was avowedly writing of a segment of a generation, which is as much as anyone can purport to do, and primarily of those young college graduates who deemed themselves intellectuals, and perhaps it may be said that he was striving to record a mood rather than to justify it. In any case, with certain amendments the passages might apply to a large section of young middle-class America. Much of it is strikingly confirmed, on a less articulate and sophisticated level, in the self-portraits of Princeton seniors contained in *The Unsilent Generation*. In a sense his portrait blended two views of what is going on; the notion, on the one hand, that it is possible—economically and every other way—to "get down to the business of living" at an early age, and the conviction that it is impossible to do anything about the larger perils of the world. Thus is *Time's* optimism happily blended with the dourness of more skeptical man; everything is serene in suburbia, and the world is way beyond us.

To ex-Socialist Dan Bell, writing in the same symposium, the matter was not quite so simple; he detected among the young an "underlying restlessness, a feeling of being cheated out of adventure, and a search for passion." But: ". . . the problem for the generation is less, I would argue, the 'fear of experience' than an inability to define an 'enemy.' One can have causes and passions only when one knows against whom to fight. The writers of the twenties—Dadaist, Menckenian and nihilist—scorned bourgeois mores. The radicals of the thirties fought 'capitalism,' Fascism and, some, Stalinism. Today, intellectually, emotionally, who is the enemy that one can fight?"

In his *Memoirs of a Revolutionist*, Dwight Macdonald, a refugee from that political nook-and-cranny known as Trotskyism and other varieties of anti-Stalinist radicalism, onetime editor of a magazine called *Politics*, summed up his own retirement from politics (large and small *p*):

"The questions that now interest me are not the 'big' ones: What to Do about Russia? Is Planning Incompatible with Capitalism? Will There Be a Depression? Does America Need a Labor Party or a Revitalized Democratic Party— or Just a Dozen More TVAs? Is World Government the Answer to the H-bomb? These seem to me either unimportant or unanswerable. So long as the dominant areas of the world are organized in vast super-states, whose economic base is large-scale industry and whose political base is tens of millions of helpless 'citizens,' I see no hope of significant improvement . . . It is the 'small' questions that now seem to me significant. What is a good life? How do we know what's good and what's bad? . . . Who am I? How can I live lovingly, truthfully, pleasurably?"

The questions with which Macdonald is now confronting himself are obviously neither inconsequential nor novel. What is interesting is the view that they are somehow more answerable than those he defines as the "big" ones, or that complete and total answers may be found outside the framework of politics. How, for example, does one define "the good life" without at least considering whether it involves a degree of social responsibility? Let him beware; someone will transform his inquiries into a sociological do-it-yourself project.

Each in his way—Podhoretz, Bell and Macdonald, one in his early thirties, the second nearing forty, the third in his fifties—describes a variety of political exhaustion. In different tones each imparts the sense that there is little that can be done, or that would prove to be worthy of the effort. The great battles are either over, or too big for us; the radicalism of another day is immaterial, irrelevant and incompetent; what is the point of carrying banners without slogans?

Many voices echo some of these notes, each expressing its own form of beatness and none perhaps as far removed as it would like to imagine from those who "in being beat" abandon "all desire to control nature, events or people" and view politics as an "arena in which Squares juggle words in a gigantic hoax based on the premise that two follows one."*

Despite the spectacle of mass settling down, the flowering of suburbia and the statistics of economic advance, there is plainly something wrong with the highly publicized image of American serenity. The beat generation may be a fragmentary, peripheral upheaval; more meaningful is the wider withdrawal and frustration. Sam Lubell, after touring the country during the 1958 elections, wrote: "One finds a deep uneasiness. This uneasiness has a curious quality. It is not fretting over something that has already happened. Mainly, it reflects an anxiety over impending disaster, a sense that as a nation we are beset by problems which are slipping beyond our control."†

The mounting traffic in tranquilizers challenges the picture of a nation enjoying its labors and resting well, even where the lawns are greenest. A study of Englewood, New Jersey, published in 1959, disclosed widespread family tensions induced by the pressures of "keeping up."

---

* Gene Feldman and Max Gartenberg in their introduction to *The Beat Generation and the Angry Young Men* (New York, Citadel Press, 1958).

† In November, Lubell reported a momentary brightening of mood, created largely by the Eisenhower-Khrushchev talk.

A dispatch by Austin C. Wehrwein to *The Times* summarized the findings this way:

CHICAGO, Aug. 7—Life in growing suburbia, specifically in Englewood, N.J., is giving people ulcers, heart attacks and other "tension-related psychosomatic disorders," according to a doctor who practices there . . .

The report was made by Dr. Richard E. Gordon and his wife, Katherine C. Gordon, after a study of admissions to the Englewood hospital.

They found that everything from crab grass to high taxes played a role in emotional difficulties that are linked to varied diseases. The cogent fact about Englewood, the report said, was that it was a fast-growing suburb with "rapid social mobility."

In plain talk this means, roughly, that many families are busy getting ahead.

How many lost dreams are summarized in that report?

It is, of course, part of the unending human self-deception to believe that a change of address may resolve all the perplexities of life, and that escape from the crowded city streets to the sunlit spaciousness of suburbia will automatically bring marital harmony and spiritual calm. The notion, indeed, that all we seek in life is peace and quiet is one of the central befuddlements of our age; is the tranquilized man the dream-figure of our century, his senses sufficiently dulled to avoid pleasure and pain and perception alike?

Nevertheless there remains a special poignancy about the failure of the suburban vision. For many of those who have made it to the outskirts have labored long to pay for the journey; that so many have found so little satisfaction in the climax of the journey cannot be simply dismissed as proof that man cannot buy heaven on earth.

But it has also become fashionable to cite the unrest in

suburbia as evidence that all our ills are those of the mind, and that any absorption with economic pressures reflects a sort of cultural lag. Even in Englewood, of course, taxes and crab grass alike shadow the model home. But far more painful is the lot of the man we like to call "average" in a time when inflation is more and more viewed as an uncombatable malignancy.

Not long ago *Pravda* expressed disbelief at the news that "the average family income" in the USA was $95 a week, as reported by the Census Bureau. *The Times* undertook to educate the Russians by selecting a family in that bracket and proving that it was typical of "many families, including those in the high-cost New York area" who "enjoy the ordinary comforts of American life while living on this amount." But the exercise was a dubious triumph. The caption under a family portrait read:

"Typical evening of leisure and relaxation in the pine-paneled basement family room. Mr. Murray reads to twenty-one-month-old Mary Elizabeth while other children play games. Mrs. Murray mends. Television set also is here. Mr. and Mrs. Murray almost never dine out or go to movies. The family budget allows for some outside entertainment for children and occasional coffe-and-cake guests."

And the article explained that "although the Murrays have no savings, they believe that Mrs. Murray's nursing profession is like money in the bank or future funds on which they can plan."

For the many Murrays, the new peaks of national well-being had brought neither high living nor money in the bank; there was only the TV set, and the rigged quiz.

Clearly, by world comparisons, the American standard of living could not be discounted as Luceian legend. But neither had it ended all economic insecurity and all man's preoccupation with the devilish uncertainties attendant upon the machinery of living for the "average man." For many if not the mass of men, "quiet desperation" was still a common characteristic.

The sense of unease was only partly related to the pressures of private budget-balancing in an inflationary age. There was, one felt, a deeper disturbance; it was simply accentuated for many by the mysteries of economics.

The condition was hardly unprecedented or unique to our day. Writing in 1929, in the months before Black Friday shattered the legend of America's economic invulnerability, Walter Lippmann in *A Preface to Morals* spoke of the crumbling of old belief, of the bleakness of "modern man's discontent":

"At the heart of it there are likely to be moments of blank misgiving in which he finds that the civilization of which he is a part leaves a dusty taste in his mouth. He may be very busy with many things, but he discovers one day that he is no longer sure they are worth doing. He has been much preoccupied, but he is no longer sure he knows why . . . It occurs to him that it is a great deal of trouble to live, and that even in the best of lives the thrills are few and far between. He begins more or less consciously to seek satisfactions, because he is no longer satisfied, and all the while he realizes that the pursuit of happiness was always a most unhappy quest."

In 1949, just two decades later, Arthur Schlesinger, Jr., was saying in *The Vital Center*:

"Western man in the middle of the twentieth century is tense, uncertain, adrift. We look upon our epoch as a time of troubles, an age of anxiety. The grounds of our civilization, of our certitude, are breaking up under our feet, and familiar ideas and institutions vanish as we reach for them . . ."

To each writer the crackup was equally real and each attempted to formulate—Lippmann in highly personal terms, Schlesinger in political discourse—some answer to the loss of nerve.

In 1959 despair moved at least one man to a modest statement of objective. "To stay sane in an insane society may indeed require the most sustained emotional and intellectual efforts that a man is capable of," wrote Lewis Coser in *Dissent*.

From one viewpoint it may be said that we are the victims of an emotional crisis that has been building up since 1914, that man has never been quite the same since the blood-drenched slaughters of the early years of World War I, and that the H-bomb is the symbol of our futility. To someone like myself born in 1915, it is hard to remember any time when reason seemed to be in the ascendancy and when we were unafflicted by existing disorder or the threat of greater catastrophe to come. I was not quite fourteen when the Depression struck America; the thirties were alternately shadowed by economic tragedy, the rise of Nazism, the victory of Fascism in Spain in what seemed like the decisive battleground of the decade, the collapse of the Russian myth in the fantasies of the Moscow trials, and the expectation of larger war.

One had hardly a moment to breathe between the surrender of Japan and the beginnings of the cold war; by 1948 the Communists had staged their coup in Czechoslovakia and shattered the illusions of multitudes of innocents, just as the Nazi-Soviet Pact had done in 1939. In 1950 we were thrust overnight into a conflict in Korea, to most Amer-

icans a remote, unreal terrain; even the knowledge that for
the first time men were fighting under the banner of the
United Nations in defense of the principle of collective security against aggression, rather than as the conscripts of
national states, could not dispel the gloom one felt at the
awareness that "here we go again." Finally—or finally, as of
this writing—there was the ruthless Russian intervention in
Hungary, where young men once again perished defying a
colossus while we wrung our hands impotently and even our
most reckless "liberationists" fled for cover.

Since 1914, then, we have lived through longer than a
forty-five-years war, and the end is not in sight. During the
same period we have wrought wonders of material progress,
and glimpsed new horizons of abundance through the prospective peaceful uses of atomic energy. But our possessions,
our gadgets, our little victories over nature look lusterless
in our hands. For, as Herblock intermittently reminds us,
The Thing is ticking; and the communiqués of the day
mock all our triumphs:

WASHINGTON (AP)—The United States may have developed
a lithium bomb—a comparatively cheap method of producing a walloping hydrogen explosion . . .

Meanwhile the air is filled with jungle noises. Columnist
Robert C. Ruark offers his formula for curbing juvenile
delinquency:

"The Mosaic law was good enough for the Biblical people
and I am getting to be strictly an eye-for-eye, tooth-for-tooth
cat myself. 'Thou shalt not kill' is a good line and, if you
do, the idea is that somebody ought to kill you right back
as swiftly as possible and with a minimum of sentiment or
excuse. If this sounds harsh, I quote the Bible and J. Edgar
Hoover as my principal teachers."

The voices of reassurance are similarly unconvincing. David Riesman suggested a few years ago that trouble was greatly exaggerated by men with a nostalgia for old political combats: ". . . our steadily rising productivity has made it possible for politicians to pay off their promises in jobs and coin of the realm rather than in a fanatical search for scapegoats . . . Despite the current outcry over apathy and corruption, Americans possess increasingly competent government, without having to spend much energy getting it. Many intellectuals and nonintellectuals feel uncomfortable in this situation and wish for parties and programs that would provide election Armageddons and 'meaningful' issues —as many once 'found such issues' by applying Marxist stereotypes to events. But here, as in the economic area, the European model has been quite misleading . . ."

Those who are less optimistic about our national equanimity urge that we turn fiercely upon ourselves, acknowledge that the universal condition of disorder lies within each man and that all political nostrums must fail because of the evil that lurks in each dark soul. It is not society that is ailing, or in the reorganization of society that we shall find any solutions; it is all of us who are sick, sick, sick; it is in therapy or theology alone that we will find peace; liberalism needs not a program but a doctor.

We have, of course, learned a good deal about ourselves in this century and much of the discovery is unpleasant. For those who clung to the vision of the perfectability of man, the disillusionment has been especially rough; for those who minimized the spasms of irrationality in man, the organized murder of Fascist and Communist states has been pitiless revelation. We have much more to learn in the whole murky realm of the private personality.

Yet none of this has quite told the whole story. Given

the history of the last forty-five years, one is almost compelled to marvel that so many men in so many places still
find a common ethical language; that such concepts as liberty, equality and fraternity still have a shared meaning;
that the capacity for heroism of a freedom fighter in Buda-
pest or a Negro school child in Little Rock still endures
as it did at Dunkirk and Madrid; that men apparently in
full possession of their wits are still capable of being moved
by considerations other than flagrant self-interest (unless the
desire to satisfy one's own conscience may be called a form
of self-gratification) or irrational sexual compulsion. Some
may choose to define this as the continuity of religious
impulse and others may simply discern in it the existence
of a moral realm; but few are totally unaware of it, or do
not at some moment in their lives identify the phenomenon.
It is not enough, it seems to me, to derogate all this by
regarding Jesus as a compulsive masochist, or charity as never
more than an expression of guilt.

On the surface this appears to be a time when any reflections related to the continuity of idealism are deemed either
naïve or, in the lingo of the politicians, "impractical." Any
militant brand of humanist liberalism is termed passé either
because, as we are told by the realistic ward heeler, the
average citizen is so well-off that he doesn't care or because,
as we are told by the disaffected intellectual, he is so beat
that he is beyond caring. Let each man, then, cultivate his
own garden in his own way, whether he believes that all is
well or that all is lost; in either case he is in no mood for
great endeavors.

Meanwhile others simply admonish us to realize that this
is necessarily a time of "limited objectives." The unalterable
fact of life is the Soviet threat to other nations; since it is
unthinkable to contemplate preventive war, we can do noth-

ing more than sit around, keep our fists up and try to concentrate on the comforts of life. This is the way things will be for a long time unless they awkwardly explode in our faces; but let it be clear that there is nothing anyone can do that matters much in a time of stalemate. Let "prudence" and "moderation" reign.

But, for some, such answers remain unsatisfying. Liberalism admittedly seems defensive, sluggish, apologetic in most of the manifestations of its public spokesmen; many of its practitioners are reminiscent of the "tired radicals" of 1919 who, as Walter Weyl wrote, had once "aspired to overturn society" and ended up "fighting in a dull Board of Directors of a village library for the inclusion of certain books." Then, as now, many had "lost faith in progress, in the rationality and disinterestedness of man, and in the malleability of society."*

Liberalism had been thus buried before. Yet it was less than fifteen years from the disenchantment of Herbert Croly —"the chief distinguishing aspect of the Presidential campaign of 1920," he wrote, "is the eclipse of liberalism or progressivism as an effective force in American politics"— to the birth of the New Deal. No iron law of history decrees that another resurgence is forever excluded.

* Quoted in *The Perils of Prosperity*, by William E. Leuchtenberg.

CHAPTER 3

The Cult of Personality

PUBLIC DISCUSSION of political candidates is increasingly reminiscent of the language employed by high-school freshmen in casting about for their class president. That may partly explain why, as kids get a little older, so many of them find themselves quite aloof from the squabbles of their elders and so uninspired by the nature of the competition they are witnessing. More and more the choice of nominees bogs down in argument over the rival intensities of sex appeal, otherwise known as "TV personality"; Freud and Gallup seem to be the arbiters of our destiny. One is far more likely to hear a candidate described as "cute" rather than great, and no word is more likely to bring pleasure to his managers.

There are times, however, when things grow hopelessly complicated when viewed in these terms. It has been widely assumed, for example, that much of Dwight D. Eisenhower's political prowess was generated by what is described as "the father image." An anxious, war-weary country was looking for Papa; there he was. The fact that Papa seemed to flee to the golf course in hours of trouble, or that, by 1956, his strong, guiding hand often proved so flabby did not seem to banish the sense of security he created by just being within reach of a telephone.

But how does one reconcile such analysis with the remarkable public appeal which the opinion polls credit to Senator Kennedy? Here is Everywoman's son, and perhaps her lover, and perhaps a mingling of both in the best modern fashion. His boyishness invites protection and solicitude; it is he who needs Mama, now considered a very important personage at the polls. And what are the ingredients that made Nelson Rockefeller an overnight political phenomenon? Did Averell Harriman fail as father? Is Rockefeller a daddy, son or romantic partner? And surely Richard Nixon, whatever else may be said about him, hardly resembles the strong man around the house, but a lot of the girls are said to go for him.

The more one ponders these varied interpretations, the larger the confusion that may ensue. Campaign managers may eventually be forced to hire teams of psychiatric aides to find out, politically speaking, who is doing what to whom, and whether they have a child or father on their hands.

I do not discount the factor of personality in politics, and the growth of the television industry has probably reduced the possibility that another Lincoln will be favored by the boys in the backroom; he would surely be the despair of the TV make-up artists. Nor do I doubt that Franklin D. Roosevelt's political successes rested on something more magnetic than that medley of brilliant improvisation known as the New Deal. By the same token, one need only recall the political disaster that befell Thomas E. Dewey in 1948 to recognize that a certain genius for creating personal hostility can take a man a long way out of politics, regardless of his technical adroitness or cold intelligence. There can be no doubt that the television camera may be quite merciless in its exposure of the unfortunate character—the unlikable man.

Nevertheless it seems to me that the mounting preoccupation with personality lays bare the fatuousness and vacuity of our political combats. Nor am I wholly prepared to concede that all the lessons of our recent history show that the secrets of personality hold the key to all the mysteries of political life.

It is quite possible that factors other than Mr. Dewey's tendency to suggest that the voters remain at a decent distance from him shaped his 1948 defeat. There is a respectable body of opinion which holds that Republican treatment of the farmers in the 1948 Congress stirred an infinitely deeper revolt than anyone had forecast; there is also statistical evidence to support the view that the civil rights plank adopted at the 1948 Democratic Convention—leading to the bolt of some diehard Southern contingents—brought Mr. Truman vital dividends in some crucial Negro areas. And so on.

There was, in short, nothing inevitable about the outcome simply because Truman had created the public portrait of "good guy" while Dewey so adroitly succeeded in offending. Similarly it is highly possible Mr. Dewey would have defeated Mr. Truman if they had been adversaries again in 1952, given the national mood and condition prevailing at that time.

Senator McCarthy offered shattering proof of how far a man can go without the mystique of TV personality, if he happens to stumble on the right subject at the right time and if the climate created by the major mass-communication media is congenial to him. McCarthy on the television screen was not exceptionally handsome, warm, witty, glib, nor was he plainly papa, son or lover; he was an unshaven ham, a brash bully, with only a remote magnetism and a furtive virility; at moments he was a caricature of a wild-eyed radical. But McCarthy clung tenaciously to an issue in which the country felt a deep involvement; he shrewdly exploited the bitterness and fears of a lot of Americans, many of whom had suffered personal loss at the hands of the Communists in the Korean war. He lied and cheated and faked, and he did so without any extraordinary gifts, but he perplexed and "sent" the nation for many months. In private he was a pretty pleasant character, but surely second-rate as political charmers go. All of that was surely less important than the accident of his encounter with a theme that touched so many nerves.

Speculation about current political figures, however, rarely identifies a man with an idea, a fighting thought, a controversial dream. It is plainly the opinion of most of the managers that such identification is to be carefully avoided. Governor Meyner of New Jersey is an especially striking example of the strategy of withdrawal. He is by all accounts an informed, thoughtful man; watching him on a "Meet the Press" television show or some variation thereof, however, he seems engaged in a calculated effort to prove that he is just a personable country boy, both too modest and too unversed in the affairs of the world to hold a strong opinion on anything except the price of eggs on New Jersey farms.

Senator Symington has voted consistently with the liberal bloc in the Senate. Nevertheless—and this is said to be his true political strength—he has managed to do so without antagonizing either conservative business interests or Dixie-crats, which is another way of saying that he has somehow managed to communicate the impression that he doesn't feel very strongly about anything. "I'm a practical liberal; I don't want to have a global stare," he told Irwin Ross in an interview. Like all "practical" men, he stands on his personality, and there are many who believe that he is the most handsome entry in the sweepstakes.

Governor Rockefeller, suffering from the awareness that many of his private views on national and world issues would be regarded as liberal heresies by the Republican Old Guard, succeeded in going through the 1958 New York gubernatorial campaign without any major references to events beyond the borders of the state of New York. He solemnly insisted that such matters were irrelevant; there were some who argued that his best chance for further success in the quest for the Presidential nomination rested on continuing this concealment, and that each time he revealed the lively functioning of his mind he exposed himself to new trouble. Rockefeller was unable to sustain the masquerade. In his travels around the country he succeeded only in convincing the Old Guard that he really wasn't one of the boys, and that beneath the bland surface lay a core of liberal convictions. By January, 1960, he felt obliged to call retreat, at least temporarily; his personality could not quite overcome the unorthodoxy of his politics in the rock-ribbed Republican set.

Senator Kennedy, who must somehow live down the silence he maintained during the difficult McCarthy period, has identified himself with the cause of union reform, and may have staked more on it than some of his sponsors consider expedient. Nevertheless what he says and does evokes far less interest than his unmistakable assets as charm boy. Kennedy's mingled intelligence and lack of visceral responses are the important things about him; but they rarely figure in public discussion about him. His hair-do (shall he wear it long or short?) appears to invite more debate than the state of his eggheadedness.

None of these men is cited as an especially stark exhibit; each merely symbolizes the prevailing style in an age when it is regarded as unfashionable and unlucky to be called a "crusader." Thus it is that Hubert Humphrey, despite some ill-fated attempts to accommodate himself to the dominant spirit, is generally written off as a presidential possibility because he is irrevocably linked with what James Reston likes to call "the extreme liberal wing" of the Democratic Party. In other words, he is suspected of strong convictions, and further hampered by his irrepressible tendency to elaborate them at length in public.

It was back in 1952 that Mr. Stevenson advanced the formula that a candidate ought to "say what he means and mean what he says" and perhaps the result of that experiment has cast a permanent pall over political behavior in our time. This is not to say that he said everything he meant or meant everything he said; but his ratio of authenticity in that year was incontestably high. And since then one has the feeling that most of the wise political men have been telling their protégés: "let that be a lesson to you." Too often in 1956 Mr. Stevenson seemed to be heeding the same admonition: beware of fidelity to oneself.

This leaves Mr. Nixon, who, unlike so many others, has rarely refused to take a stand but has, instead, shifted from side to side without any betrayal of self-consciousness. But that is so fascinating an exhibit of the strategy of noncommitment that, like Hubert Humphrey's contrary adventure, it is a separate story.

Implicit in all of this is the sense that, despite all the personality contests, politics has acquired a soporific dullness.

At times one feels as if the productions should be staged at Atlantic City; we are picking Mr. America. How shall we persuade our children to care?

In an essay called "Triumph of the Smooth Deal," Karl Meyer, writing from Washington for *Commentary* magazine in 1959, noted that "the absence of passion and purpose in American politics, despite the stimulus of domestic and world crises, is a dismaying reality . . . In the twilight years of the Eisenhower administration it is especially melancholy to contemplate a Congress where dissonance is muted in the interests of avoiding a 'controversial' stand."

In a time that ought to be characterized by great debate, the most notable thing about our political dialogue is the vast area of issues deemed virtually undiscussible.

One recalls with incredulity how easy it was in 1956 for Mr. Eisenhower to bury Mr. Stevenson's plea for cessation of H-bomb tests. Eventually the issue was to rise again; but not until long after a national campaign in which this surely should have been a major topic. After all, it involved nothing more nor less than the question of survival.

But if the matter of the bomb transcends—or should—all other public controversy, its burial is hardly an isolated instance of the muting of serious debate.

At any moment of any day or night, the Chinese Communists may decide to risk everything either in a frontal attack on Formosa or in a preliminary attempt to seize the offshore islands of Quemoy and Matsu. This would confront American policy makers with perhaps the gravest decision of our century. It would also be an intolerable decision; for the choice might well lie between the launching of atomic counterattack or craven surrender of a position to which we have recklessly committed ourselves.

The possibility that such a choice may be thrust upon us

will continue to exist so long as the deadlock over Formosa remains unbroken. It can only be broken—if at all—by revaluation of our whole position with respect to Communist China. The most responsible solution advanced, and one which most of our allies in the world would welcome, involves the creation of a United Nations trusteeship for Formosa. This, in turn, would mean official abandonment of Chiang's dream of a triumphant return to the Chinese mainland under the cover of American guns. It would probably also mean the recognition of Red China.

There is no assurance that Peking would accept this formula. We shall never find out until we advance it. At the very least our advocacy of such a course would promptly and dramatically shift moral responsibility for any Far Eastern crisis to the commissars. But we are so bedeviled by the political sloganry of the last decade that we shrink from any significant national discussion of the alternatives. The Committee of 1,000,000 issues periodic manifestos decrying any hint of modification in our China policy. Senators and Congressmen either ritualistically attach their names to such declarations or nervously look the other way. As far as most of the editorial pages of the nation are concerned, the danger simply does not exist—except in those interludes when the Communist guns step up their shelling of Quemoy and Matsu, calling forth bursts of retaliatory fire from typewriters throughout our land.

Perhaps the Communists will indefinitely withhold the blow. Possibly they will wait for Chiang's death and the attrition of his regime. The point is that the initiative is theirs so long as the present stalemate obtains; they are quite literally the masters of our fate. It is, I submit, dumb diplomacy to remain trapped in such a corner unless and until every honorable means of escape has been attempted. We persist in a national policy most fittingly symbolized by the late Mr. Dulles' ban on American newspaper coverage of the Chinese mainland. We shall act as if they are not there and, if we act that way long enough and persistently enough, they will go away. Meanwhile, silence, please. How can any effective disarmament program be contemplated without the participation of Red China? The question is neither widely asked nor clearly answered.

A similar diffidence surrounds our relations with Western Germany. Many responsible Western statesmen are known to believe that any stabilization in Europe is implausible so long as we insist upon Western Germany's enlistment in NATO. It is their contention that only a drastic revision of our German policy, based upon the goal of a free, unified, *neutralized* Germany, offers any foundation for fruitful negotiation. There are obvious defects as well as merits in the theory, even assuming that our acceptance of it would make the Russians more amenable to a larger settlement. It is argued that West Germany's withdrawal from NATO would make the West more dependent than ever before on nuclear arms in the event of a European clash. But the logic of our position was virtually removed when the President himself asserted that any explosion resulting from the Berlin crisis would not under any circumstances be confined to ground troops. If it is our view, as the President suggests, that any war in Europe will be nuclear war, there is compelling reason for re-examination of our German position.

Whether I am right or wrong in these assessments, it is surely fantastic that there is so little argument about the rights or wrongs of this critique. In the same context it is equally grotesque that the American decision to share atomic know-how with Germany was ratified by Congress without any full-dress debate, with only a few scattered expressions of guarded apprehension, and with only a handful of dissenting editorial comments. Less than fifteen years after V-E Day, Dr. Adenauer's Western Germany had achieved an immunity from American criticism approaching that enjoyed by Chiang Kai-shek, and any alteration of policy that might be resented by *Der Alte* was barred from the agenda until the death of Mr. Dulles. Our proper admiration for Berlin's resistance to the Communist thrust assumes an almost fawning tone. We now bestow on the West Germans some of the uncritical adulation we had reserved for the Russians during the wartime alliance, and skepticism is frequently denounced as a threat to "Western unity."

One should be able to appreciate the efforts of decent democrats in Germany to atone for the horrors of Hitler without acting as if Germany had overnight become the savior of free man and Dr. Adenauer the hope of the Western world. But we seem incapable of "moderation" in our international romances, much as we enshrine it at home.

The list of undebatables and unmentionables is long. To many young men and women the quality of nondebate which accompanied the latest Congressional vote extending the draft for four years must have been peculiarly disheartening. Here is an issue which shadows the lives of a whole emerging generation. Competent military opinion has repeatedly argued that, in this transformed era, the concept of mass conscription has become obsolete; that the national defense would be far better served—as Mr. Stevenson proposed in 1956—by a trained, professional, better-paid Army equipped for the special missions of a very special situation. The British have moved with some success in exactly that direction.

Again one may acknowledge that the argument is not simple. But surely it is serious, and deserving of extended reflection. What actually happened in Congress was that a handful of men aired their doubts, a few pleaded that the extension of the draft be limited to two years rather than four, and the original proposal was overwhelmingly approved after what might be generously called a mumble of debate.

Shortly thereafter there were certain disclosures about the Army's tendency to use G.I.'s as chauffeurs and men-around-the-house for the Army brass and there was a mild flurry of indignation, but that, too, quickly passed.

As far as 99 percent of the editorial writers were concerned, the draft was simply beyond argument. They had brushed off the Stevenson proposal in 1956, just as they had spurned his call for suspension of H-bomb testing, with the contempt they reserve for ordinary mortals who quarrel with generals, and they displayed little interest now in a legislative act that insured four more years of conscription.

The controversy really was all over before it began, and any young men who wondered whether they would truly render maximum service to their country by going through the motions of basic training could continue to wonder; theirs was not to reason why.

In surveying the political no man's land one must also see the infinite capacity for survival displayed by such agencies as the House Un-American Activities Committee and the Senate Internal Security Committee. Relentlessly they pursue the faded foe that domestic Communism has become; the spirit of their endeavors was voiced by Senator Goldwater (R-Ariz.) in July, 1959, when he proclaimed: "I am not willing to accept the idea that there are no Communists left in this country; I think that if we lift enough rocks, we will find some." So the rock-lifting went on; all the "economizers" on both sides of the aisle were invariably able to find funds for these exercises, and discretion dictated that no personable aspirant for the Presidency get caught in a fracas involving the sanctity of the works of Congressman Francis Walter of Pennsylvania, head of the House committee, or Senator James Eastland of Mississippi, head of its Senate counterpart.

As for the press, it had long ago lost any zest for combat with these seekers-after-subversion. It had fallen on its face when its most exalted and respected pillar—the *New York Times*—had come under Mr. Eastland's fire, and, after that collapse, no surrender could seem too large. (The gruesome details of this and other aspects of the press performance are given in a subsequent chapter.)

Meanwhile the personality contest went on, heading into the climactic days of 1960. The Gallup polls continued; but the debate was blurred and cautious. Would any man rise above the dullness? Surely some man better than Joe Mc-Carthy ought to be able, in this cruel time, to find an equally stimulating but less synthetic issue than he found, and perhaps to evoke some of the nobler emotions some Americans felt when Mr. Stevenson was giving the American Legion a lecture on know-nothingism eight years ago, or when Franklin Delano Roosevelt was telling a frightened, despairing populace that we had "nothing to fear but fear itself."

CHAPTER 4

The Liberal Retreat

"WITH THE Democratic victory in the 1948 elections, American liberalism returned to power. It had been in eclipse (even though nominally in office) for nearly a decade—its decline began with the outbreak of war in 1939 and reached its low point with the Republican sweep of 1946. Now, suddenly, exile was over, the conservatives were routed, and a new crew of liberal militants catapulted into office."

So wrote Irwin Ross in *Strategy for Liberals* early in 1949, in the jubilant aftermath of Harry Truman's remarkable triumph over Thomas E. Dewey and Dr. Gallup, and the Democratic Congressional landslide that accompanied his victory.

"In a major sense, the election altered the relationship of political forces in America," Ross continued. "Organized liberalism emerged with a strength, a mandate and an opportunity unmatched since 1933. The nation had unmistakably swung to the left. But is the left equal to the tasks imposed on it? Has it a program commensurate with its responsibilities? Has it the will and the power to realize the promises implicit in its rhetoric—can it end the threat of depression, eliminate poverty, build a society as democratic in its economic relations as in its political forms? Can the Fair Deal succeed where the New Deal failed?"

The hopes were high, the challenge seemed clear. Now we are all more than a decade older, perhaps a trifle wiser and, looking back over the ten years that have elapsed, we may well ponder how the opportunities were squandered, the "mandate" so largely ignored.

In part, of course, the optimism was unjustified by reality. The voting returns were plain enough; the scope of the liberal gain was massive. But Mr. Truman was something less than a resolute, adventurous liberal crusader; it was hard to detect in him any deep impulses of Wilsonian idealism or the tough-minded pragmatism of Franklin D. Roosevelt. He could gruffly pay his rhetorical respects to progressive legislation but he was neither creative nor original in this realm; he was, one might say, a radical George Babbitt. In the early years of his Administration he betrayed an insistent distrust of any men who came bearing unconventional ideas; he was as apt as any backward Republican to view such characters as "longhairs," and the exodus of New Dealers from government began soon after he took office. Not until late—too late—in his Administration did he begin to suspect that there was no fatal contradiction between brain power and political power.

This was most painfully true of his conduct of domestic affairs. Harry Truman was the product of a rough political machine; he knew it, and reveled in the knowledge, and many of the ultimate misfortunes of his Administration are traceable to his tendency to let the standards of the political clubhouse prevail in the higher echelons of government.

Such a man was hardly likely to inspire a younger generation or to impart new dimensions of nobility and purpose to the cause of liberalism.

But Mr. Truman was also the victim of circumstances beyond his control. The Communist aggression that began in Korea in June, 1950, destroyed any chance for domestic innovation; it also placed his Administration in an even more defensive posture with respect to the Communist issue at home. One might say that Mr. Truman spent his last two years in office leading the democratic resistance to a Communist assault abroad while seeking to prove to his countrymen that he was neither a captive nor agent of Communism at home. Much of the American press never fully perceived or acknowledged the irony.

His response to the Korean crisis was instinctive, courageous and unwavering, just as had been his conduct when the Russian threat to Greece and Turkey became acute in 1947. In these great moments, and in his espousal of such efforts as the Point Four program for American aid to underprivileged nations, Truman rose far above the humdrum political community which spawned him, and achieved an authentic place in history. But a recognition of these achievements scarcely justifies the fashioning of any legend of Truman as liberal leader. In subsequent years it has been commonplace to identify the attack on our domestic freedoms with the name of Senator McCarthy. Let it not be forgotten, however, that the federal loyalty program and all the cruel excesses associated with it began in the time of Mr. Truman; that the notorious Smith Act prosecutions—in which we found ourselves prosecuting men not for what they did but for what they dreamed of doing—were undertaken by Attorney General Tom Clark in the same epoch under a statute approved by Franklin D. Roosevelt.

Whatever his virtues and vices, Mr. Truman was a robust, spirited figure who labored long and hard in a world he never made. But he was incapable of giving continuity or new direction to the movement of liberalism.

By the end of 1952 the visions of resurgence had crumbled. Adlai Stevenson campaigned valiantly and unconventionally, creating a sense that there was a new voice abroad in the land. To many young men and women, his campaign that year must seem like their last encounter with the wine of political idealism. Time and again Stevenson said what he believed in places where it seemed least expedient for him to do so; the style of his campaign was set in his plea for dissent before the American Legion.

No doubt Stevenson's defeat helped shape the cynicism and withdrawal that marked the years immediately afterward. No one can state with any confidence that any candidate could have defeated Dwight D. Eisenhower that year. The yearning for change was nation-wide; the build-up of Eisenhower as savior represented the best promotion campaign that money could buy; Stevenson told a country weary of hot war in Korea and cold war in the world that there were no quick and easy solutions—and many Americans preferred to believe there were. Eisenhower countered Stevenson's profound sense of doubt with the clichés of certainty. The scandals that beset the Truman Administration plagued Stevenson throughout the long autumn. They were deftly exploited by such apostles of rectitude as Sherman Adams and they confronted Stevenson with the insoluble dilemma of defending or disowning the stains of a Democratic era.

With Stevenson's defeat came demoralization in many liberal areas. Was it possible, men began to ask anew, that he was "too good" for our kind of politics? Was it possible that no man could successfully "talk sense" to the American people; did his failure mean that humility to the point of self-deprecation was a fatal disqualification for public office? Would any man be able to overcome the massive, concentrated power of television and press once the White House was occupied by a Republican—any Republican? Had the McCarthy distortion of liberalism captivated so large a section of the electorate that no man suspected of liberal associations could function effectively in the political arena? Was labor leadership so alienated from its members that it could no longer be taken seriously as a political force?

Such were some of the morose meditations that gripped the liberal community as the magnitude of Stevenson's loss became apparent. The mood of defeatism was lightened for some, of course, by the great expectations promoted by the Eisenhower publicists. He had, after all, won the nomination after a bitter struggle with the conservative troops rallied under the Taft banner. He was generally depicted as a man of good will and generous impulse; the image of him as a pillar of decency had been sufficiently strong to persuade some liberals four years earlier that he would make an exemplary candidate on the Democratic ticket.

But the weakness and irresolution he soon manifested in combat—or noncombat—with McCarthy dimmed these extravagant hopes. The strongest case that had been made for him by such able supporters as August Heckscher, Jr., then chief editorial writer of the *Herald Tribune* and articulate spokesman of "modern Republicanism" in the pages of that journal, was that Eisenhower's election would somehow cool the passions and smother the prejudices stirred by the McCarthy crusade. But for nearly two years the White House time and again retreated under fire.

Men continued to say "Ike is a good guy" but the evidence mounted that he was unlikely to produce anything new in any sphere. Democrats generally capitulated to what they accepted to be the tone of the times. They shunned new ideas, shared in the general levity about eggheads and increasingly tried to prove that they were as respectable and uncreative as their adversaries.

Stagnation and stalemate seemed to be the essential characteristics of political life. There was a flurry of excitement when the President appeared likely to bow out of the 1956 race after a succession of physical reversals; but the political medicine men and the specialists agreed that a second term would be entirely consistent with his rehabilitation, especially if conducted in large measure on the playing fields of Augusta. Most of the press obediently accepted the dictum that there was no office more hospitable to convalescence than the Presidency, particularly when the patient happened to be a Republican.

And Mr. Stevenson himself, cursed by history with the misfortune of running twice against the nation's great-white-father symbol, never quite recaptured in 1956 the style and spirit of his first campaign. Many of his advisors were plainly convinced that a repetition of his lofty tactics would be disastrous; he was counseled to concentrate on such bread-and-butter issues as the high cost of living, but unhappily the Democrats were no more prepared than the Republicans to advocate the kind of economic controls that might have given meaning to the debate. I have been told that Stevenson's own disposition was to stress the failures and follies of Administration foreign policy; but his bold call for the suspension of nuclear tests was viewed with dismay by most of "the pros." Given the level of press behavior and the comatose state of much of the nation, it is questionable whether anything Stevenson could have done would have substantially reduced the margin of defeat. It is also ques-

tionable whether any man could repeat what was indisput-
ably Stevenson's moral victory of 1952; four years later the
originality of phrase and manner that distinguished his initial effort had acquired a familiar sound; it was as if his fresh
words had already become cliché.

Then, suddenly, the Eisenhower honeymoon ended. It was
not that his second term was much more conspicuously lacking in vigor or enterprise than his first. His surrenders to
McCarthy and his equivocation in the battle for civil rights
had all occurred before his re-election. But there were differences now. To the orthodox Republican commentators
and politicos who had so long protected a prize property,
Eisenhower now ceased to be indispensable; there could be
no third term. A press that had been so often muted in
deference to the sanctity of the symbol began to murmur
querulously. Yet there may well have been deeper meaning
in the steady collapse of the Eisenhower mythology. I can
hardly document the point, but it is my profound suspicion
that, by the time of the 1958 Congressional elections, Dwight
D. Eisenhower had become something of a fabulous—if still
beloved—bore.

I know it was said in many places that the gale which
swept so many Republicans out of office was in no way
aimed at the President; conceivably he would have done
better than many of his fallen brethren if his name had
appeared on the ballot. The fact remains that he pleaded
plaintively and at length for a Republican sweep; he matched
Mr. Nixon in his prophecies of the socialist doom that a
Democratic success would bring; he fully and freely associated himself with the cause of each Republican stalwart, as
well as with the most ancient economic doctrines of Hoover
Republicanism. In the course of this exercise he finally laid
to rest the illusion that there was any serious link between

Mr. Eisenhower and what some of his more liberal adherents have described as "Eisenhower Republicanism." He gave his all to the Republican flag, and it was not enough. Many suggested—as the President himself tried to do—that the result was in no way a repudiation of the Eisenhower Administration, which seemed like another way of saying that Mr. Eisenhower could not be held accountable for any of the policies and programs of the government he nominally headed.

The Democratic breakthrough was spectacular; the Republican rout was almost total. New York State was one of the few places where the trend was reversed, but there was little comfort for the Republican faithful in this news. Nelson Rockefeller had assiduously withheld any commitment to national or international Republican policies; he steadfastly insisted on discussing "state issues" alone and, when he finally and reluctantly accepted the insistent embrace of Mr. Nixon, he did so in the manner of a girl who decides to be seduced only because she knows that rape can create so ugly a scene.

To judge by nearly all the public evidence, liberalism and independence had carried the day, and most of the liberal communiqués had a tone of exultation reminiscent of the dancing in the streets of 1948.

Yet on the morning after the binge, there appeared good reason to re-examine the premises of the celebration. The truth was that despite all the battles won, all the outposts captured, all the conservatives vanquished, the condition of anything that might be described as a movement of organized liberalism in the U.S.A. was inescapably poor. Many individual politicians who called themselves liberal had won elections; but were there any sure signs that their triumphs constituted something more memorable than a big day in their own lives?

On the one hand the leadership of the Democratic Congressional delegation continued to rest in the hands of Senator Lyndon Johnson and Congressman Sam Rayburn, the two Texans who have long prided themselves on their ability to repress what they deem the excessive militancy of such men as Hubert Humphrey and Paul Douglas. There was no indication that either Johnson or Rayburn interpreted the results as any form of rebuke to their long records of passivity and their quiet partnership with Mr. Eisenhower. Mr. Eastland of Mississippi retained his seat, his seniority and his chairmanship of a major Senate committee; so did others only a trifle less obnoxious and clamorous in their confidence that they belonged to a master race. Johnson himself was described by columnist William S. White, who has long served as carrier of the Johnson message to the masses, as still entirely convinced that "the quiet tone and the centrist policy are the facts of political life."

In its first meeting after the election the Democratic National Committee vigorously declared its adherence to the cause of civil rights. But it was noted that the resolution was adopted, as one delegate put it, only because some agressive fellows insisted upon presenting it; such moguls as Carmine DeSapio and Jake Arvey carefully withheld any rhetoric in support of the pronouncement and there was a general feeling that many others would have preferred to abstain from this affront to the Southern contingent if they had not been caught in a public place. It would have at the very least been premature to say that the Democratic Party had overnight overcome its two-headedness and become a purposeful party of reinvigorated liberalism.

The liberal landscape did not appear too much more promising when one scrutinized the state of Americans for Democratic Action. At the time of its formation in 1947

ADA was widely heralded as the beginning of a momentous liberal-labor coalition, designed not only to frustrate the Communist effort to infiltrate and manipulate American liberalism but to provide the base for a major new political thrust by independent liberal and union forces. Because of the identity of many of its founding fathers, ADA was often called a "government in exile"; it was heavily populated with former New Dealers who had found life uncongenial in the aggressively anti-intellectual atmosphere of the early Truman regime. That ADA had recorded significant achievements in its decade of existence was beyond dispute. But that it had fallen far short of the expectations of its creators was equally clear.

Certainly it had swiftly and decisively attained (with the help of some monumental Communist blunders at home and abroad) one of its avowed objectives. It was a leading factor in the rout of the U.S. Communist movement in the 1948 campaign; it was instrumental in unfolding the truth about the last major domestic Communist enterprise—the Communist-run Progressive Party which bewitched Henry Wallace into running as its candidate for president. Probably ADA did more than any other single agency to expose the frauds and the fallacies, the double-think and double standards through which the Communists tried to entrap American liberals in the late 1940's as they had in the mid-1930's.

This was a solid accomplishment, too often cynically forgotten by those who have tried to depict ADA as a creature of sly subversion. But it was predominantly a negative triumph designed to pave the way for the emergence of an affirmative political vehicle. There have been fewer positive victories.

It was a caucus organized and run by ADA that was primarily responsible for the success of Hubert Humphrey's

fight for a clear-cut civil rights plank at the 1948 Democratic Convention; ADA leaders played key parts in organ-
izing the effort and ADA adherents did much of the hard,
feverish work that ultimately confounded the professionals—
including Mr. Truman himself—on the convention floor.
(It is not often remembered that Mr. Truman's Missouri
delegation and Vice-Presidential nominee Barkley's Kentucky
bloc voted unanimously against the rebellion that ultimately
contributed so much to national Democratic victory.)

ADA may similarly boast that it spoke out clearly and
forthrightly against McCarthyism at a time when respectable
political leaders were finding all manner of excuses for
maintaining an undignified silence. On this and a number
of other issues ADA has provided the stimulus of a sort of
American Fabian Society. It has also provided an initial
home for a number of men who were seeking entry into
political life but found themselves temporarily thwarted by
the condition of the political machines in their areas. It has
given them support, encouragement, a platform from which
to speak, a refuge to which they could turn. Without ADA
American politics would have been far duller and shallower
than it has been during this time of accommodation.

I neither discount nor deride what ADA has done, especially in contrast with the disorganized futility and studied
inertia that have pervaded much of both the intellectual and
labor world. Yet now, somewhat more than a decade after
its birth, ADA still looms infinitely larger in the dark imag-
inings of its critics than it does in real life. I do not like
to deprive liberals of the sense of absolute power they may
fleetingly experience when they read William Buckley's or
Westbrook Pegler's or David Lawrence's accounts of ADA's
dominance of the politics and culture of the country; but

there is a day of reckoning for all forms of self-deception. The unhappy truth is that, as of the moment of the liberal landslide of 1958, ADA still bore little resemblance to the massive liberal-labor alliance envisaged by its founders. It had signally failed to inspire the allegiance of any substantial number of young men and women; its undergraduate affiliate—Students for Democratic Action—seemed to be forever quarreling with what it regarded as the hand of restraint imposed by the elders. ADA has become primarily a meeting ground for those with sentimental ties to the liberal and radical past, a sort of Alumni Association that recruits too few of its members from more recent liberal classes.

In the course of its lifetime it has enrolled at one time or another—but not simultaneously—upward of 50,000 Americans, and successfully solicited the sympathy of a good many more for particular projects. In the old house-ad line of the liberal weeklies, its influence has been far greater than the subscription rolls would indicate; it has put more ideas in currency than its revenue would seem to permit; it has stimulated serious public debates in a time hostile to candid controversy. It has also exercised a very effective veto power on the ambitions of numerous political careerists whose records it has systematically exposed. If there were those who feared that ADA's endorsement might somehow be prejudicial to them, there were others who had learned that ADA could effectively draw distinctions that many independent voters recognized.

With all of that, ADA could not be described in that 1958 hour of national liberal triumph as the fulfillment of its founders' dream. Although it had many individual members in California and some other western states, it had few flourishing chapters west of the Mississippi. It had been increasingly unable to secure the public blessing of well-known political figures, including many who felt a sense of identity with its program. It had received steadily less, rather than more, financial support from major labor unions; David Dubinsky, Walter Reuther, Jim Carey (and Hugo Ernst until his death) have been almost alone in the constancy of their devotion.

Certain obvious explanations for its lack of size immediately occur. Not being a political party on its own, it leads a life of strange uncertainty in almost any area in which it takes root. Its primary objective in most areas has been to wrest leadership of the Democratic Party from old-line hacks and pave the way for the kind of liberal coups that have taken place in numerous states. The paradox of all this is that success in such ventures often means the liquidation of the ADA machinery. In Minnesota, for example, Humphrey and Governor Orville Freeman were early ADA leaders; Humphrey was its national co-chairman. But once the forces gathered around them had won control of the Minnesota Democratic Party, the prevailing view was that there was no longer any excuse for the continued existence of ADA in that state. And there is no ADA there now, although both Senator Humphrey and Governor Freeman continue to give active support to the national organization.

If the same drama were enacted on a national scale, it might be plausibly argued that there really was no reason for ADA to remain in business as a separate entity. But plainly that has not happened. It is unlikely to happen in the foreseeable future. Nevertheless ADA's national effectiveness is undoubtedly vitiated by its lack of any effective organization in exactly those states—Wisconsin is another example —in which men associated with it have made their largest political impression. Philadelphia, whose Mayor Dilworth has never felt obliged to veil his ADA connections, is one of the few regions where political success has not been fatal to the institutional strength of the ADA organization. But that is partly attributable to the fact that the victories of Dilworth and Senator Joseph Clark have not seriously altered the character of the Democratic machine.

Granted the complexities created by ADA's own schizoid structure—neither political party nor formal caucus within either party—its difficulties cannot be that easily defined. More basically they are the product of three major tendencies in recent years; the McCarthy assault, the cult of "moderation" which developed in its aftermath, and the flight from politics that has been at least partially induced by those phenomena.

That ADA could have been effectively smeared as "pro-Communist" or "soft on Communism" is, among other things, a commentary on the sad incapacity and/or mendacity of a large section of the U.S. press in the long night of the McCarthy miseries. Here was an organization conceived in important measure as a counteroffensive against the Communist drive at a moment when the American Communist movement was displaying its last signs of real life. It put the Communists out of business in many places. But since it was no less hostile to the intolerance of the McCarthy dogma than it was to the Communist brand of totalitarianism, it swiftly evoked the combined fury of Messrs. McCarthy, Nixon and all their lesser imitations. It was a major whipping boy of the 1952 campaign because some of Mr. Stevenson's close associates—among them Arthur Schlesinger, Jr., and Wilson Wyatt—had undeniable ADA links. And it was never quite the same after the 1952 debacle. Though it is hard to see how Eisenhower could have been defeated, the "pros" eagerly selected ADA as their scapegoat and the amateurs were never quite capable of answering back.

It seems to me far from demonstrated that ADA is in truth the "kiss of death" to any aspiring politician, as the backroom strategists like to contend. One would need far more detailed study of individual races to determine whether an ADA endorsement hurts a candidate more than it helps him, as so many Democrats have now concluded. That many of them believe this is beyond dispute; but what they really believe, I think, is not that the initials ADA are anathema to the voters but that the spirit of forthright liberalism which its initials evoke is somehow irreconcilable with the needs of ambitious Democratic candidates.

To the conventional political animal, ADA somehow signifies "trouble." It does not understand what Mr. Nixon would call the "rules of the game." It is "impractical," and darn near starry-eyed. And too often, perhaps, many of us in ADA have suffered from increasing inhibitions in public statement and speech precisely because this attack has been so widespread and unrelenting. Fearful of losing all contact with those whom it helped into public office, the organization has sometimes remained silent when it should have spoken out, failed to exploit issues that eventually became great popular campaigns, muffled positions that were deemed "embarrassing" by particular candidates.

But I do not intend to add my voice to those who seek to blame the frustrations of liberal man on the ineptitudes or inadequacies of ADA. Rather I think the moment is approaching for a full-scale reappraisal of whether the present political divisions in the country make any sense, and whether there can be any great liberal revival so long as liberalism remains essentially wedded to that divided house called the Democratic Party.

In *A Democrat Looks at His Party*, Dean Acheson offered a quiet case for the continued duality of the Democratic organization:

The most conservative leaders in the party come from the South. This sometimes causes impatience among Northern liberals. But Southern conservatism is an invaluable asset. It gives assurance that all interests and policies are weighed and considered within the party before interparty issues are framed.

This is an elegant but unconvincing rationale for the continuance of an alliance that has lost nearly all validity. In an age when the quest for human equality has become our central domestic concern, this union of incompatibles becomes increasingly grotesque. The Democratic condition is rendered worse by the theory advanced in some places that the Party must woo back those legions of conservative Catholic voters who began to defect as far back as 1940, and whose symbol of rectitude remains Joe McCarthy.

Liberals are often accused of displaying a fatal nostalgia for the simplicities of the struggles of the 1930's. Yet the desire to re-create the past is actually stronger among those Democratic traditionalists who yearn for a revival of the Roosevelt coalition and fail to understand that the new issues of a new day make such a revival implausible.

And before I am quoted out of context, let me hasten to add that I am not proposing a mass expulsion of Southern Democrats and Northern Catholics from Democratic ranks. There are many Southern Democrats groping earnestly for an honorable resolution of the desegregation conflict; some of them are taking far greater personal risks in the battle for decency than any Northern liberal. Similarly, there is no evidence that the Catholic vote is a monolithic mass of conservatism; there were eminent Catholics resisting McCarthyism long before many men of other faiths had found their voices; on economic issues the Catholic vote in Congress is generally more liberal than the Protestant.

But we will have nothing truly recognizable as a liberal movement as long as disingenuousness remains the fashion of our politics, and independent liberals remain aloof from ADA because "it has been smeared." Neither will we make honest men of our political spokesmen as long as they must live two lives. I have no vested interest in ADA's continuance, and neither do most of the men who give their time and energy without mundane reward to the service of the organization. But I suspect that if it did not exist it would have to be invented, even for the small number who give it active support and the larger number who derive some sense of relationship with political society from the fact of its existence.

We live in a time when most of our best political men—whether they call themselves Republicans, as John Sherman Cooper does, or Democrats, as Hubert Humphrey does—are torn and troubled because the circumstances of our politics prevent them from being true to themselves. Such men will never be able to live with themselves in full harmony as long as the unrealistic division endures. I am aware of the argument that a clear-cut political realignment would create the peril of French fragmentation. But I am not awed by the danger. It seems to me we are paying far too high a price for the alleged stability we have achieved under a system in which hypocrisy and deceit are the required rituals of political behavior.

My own view is that ADA and liberals generally ought

to take off all the gloves, even at the expense of divorcement from some political luminaries, and dedicate themselves to forcing a showdown within the Democratic Party. Conceivably only the threat of a third party effort could achieve that result and, as the disastrous Wallace experiment proved, such a threat has no meaning unless it has the support of organized labor. But it seems to me the proposition is worthy of consideration by any labor leader who takes a serious view of politics.

What I have ultimately in view is not the emergence of two monolithic political organisms imposing rigid "party discipline" on their members. Such a concept is an absurdity in America. I do visualize a political upheaval in which men of broadly parallel ideas would find themselves in the same structure, capable of communicating with each other and feeling something more than Senatorial courtesy about each other's ideas. Within the broadly defined categories of "liberal" and "conservative," men would, I think, find their identities. It might even be said that each party would still represent a coalition, but each coalition would be united by certain recognizable common denominators of belief.

At the moment there is unquestionably a vastly higher percentage of liberal strength within the Democratic Party. Yet the grip of the Southern bloc daily dilutes that strength. In an age when the conflict over civil rights has become so central to our political future, I do not exclude the possibility, dim though it may seem at this time, of a complete reshuffling in which the Republican Party would become the vehicle of liberal political endeavor. Indeed, such a possibility would be far less remote if it were not for the total failure of the Republicans to make any serious effort to enfranchise the Southern Negro, and to make his enfranchisement a turning point in Southern politics. Many factors may contribute to this paralysis, perhaps most important of all the continuance of the unspoken but continuing arrangement between conservative Northern Republicans and Southern Democrats that dominates so much of the business of Congress and provides so many comforts and conveniences for those on both sides. But the architects of this nonaggression pact are not immortal, and younger men may eventually refuse to extend it.

When I write of labor's participation in a political realignment, it is with full awareness of the decline of labor's status in the electoral wars. Indeed, any mature labor leadership ought to re-examine critically the self-imposed alienation of many of the large unions from ADA—and imagine what ADA might have been if it had had full-fledged labor support.

For in fact labor has found itself increasingly isolated from the independent electorate and, on occasion, from its own rank and file. Too often in the past many chieftains of labor have looked derisively at the liberal movement, as if suggesting that the eggheads were pretty innocent fellows who had never met a union payroll and could not conceivably matter much on the battlefields of politics. But recent American experience—bulwarked by events in Britain—may hint at a reverse truth: that labor, especially in its latterday condition of power and bureaucratization, has lost touch with those segments of public idealism which are vital to its effectiveness in the political arena.

Too many people have come to believe, with some documentation, that "the big union" is now as contemptuous of any large public interest as the entrenched corporation, and that much of our inflationary problem represents a tacit conspiracy between these organized forces.

When an industry-union wage agreement results in a sudden, arbitrary increase in the price of milk, many thousands are caught in what they justly view as a squeeze; but no union voice is raised to ask whether the price rise is warranted or even to acknowledge that the price of milk has any relevance to the union's operations. It is such episodes, duplicated annually in so many areas, that incite the cry of "a plague on both your houses."

I happen to think the equation is often too capriciously drawn, and that corporate power, bulwarked by the massive propaganda institutions at its command, is too carelessly linked to the strength of the union machines. But neither can I lightly discount the wide areas in which "business unionism" finds itself in daily collusion and cohabitation with the industry in which it happens to be located, and utterly unmindful of the larger considerations which ought to unite it with both the disorganized of the North and the disfranchised of the South.

Once upon a time the labor movement was the catalyst of the strongest idealistic emotions in our society. It produced noble exhibits of selflessness and sacrifice; in the primitivism of industrial conflict, unions brought dignity to thousands of individual lives, and a sense of moral values to the economic jungle. Now there are too few moments when that tradition is reaffirmed. Although multitudes of workers—especially in the South—remain unorganized, too many of labor's giants now seem as dedicated to business as usual as the men they meet across the bargaining table, and as hostile to innovation. Admittedly out of the Auto Workers Union has come a Walter Reuther, just as Paul Hoffmann emerged from the auto industry, each apparently capable of seeing beyond the narrow horizons of the contract negotiation. But such innovators are rare indeed on either side. It is not the corruption and double-dealing unveiled by the McClellan committee that matters most; such phenomena are partially symptoms of the *nouveau riche* union bloc; they can be overcome. Far more consequential is the loss of spirit among those who have never been bought. Jimmy Hoffa is a shabby vulgarization of unionism; yet in a sense he has filled a vacuum created by the general decline of union morale. The politics of labor is, by and large, suffering from the same facelessness and aimlessness that pervade the old party organizations.

Should a reinvigorated liberal-labor alliance prevail within the Democratic Party, this might well mean the launching of a third-party project by the disaffected Dixiecrats. To that possibility one can only respond that the last time a Democrat reached the White House it was in the face of two third-party movements, one sponsored by the Dixiecrats and the other by the Communists. There is some reason to doubt that the South will risk all its perquisites of Congressional seniority by another comparable rebellion. But we should not be intimidated by the prospect of a bolt, for it is probably only such a cleavage that can pave the way for more authentic political alignments.

As long as the present soggy stalemate lasts, as long as many men feel that the muddle way is the road to the White House, as long as ADA is viewed as a band of pariahs by many figures in the Democratic community, one will find it difficult to tell the beat generation that it ought to stop pouting and start shouting. Perhaps it is entirely healthy and even defensible for many middle-aged men to devote all their days and nights to contemplation of their Presidential chances, even in this agonized interval. They have, after all, but one life to give for the Presidency. But that is hardly any reason for the rest of us to let their ordeal govern our lives.

I know this will be viewed as extremist talk in some places. Unfortunately, the center has become so thronged that one can hardly recognize the faces in the crowd. In 1949 Arthur Schlesinger, Jr., wrote with grand expectations of the emergence of a "vital center," alternately known as "the non-Communist left," in the U.S.A. But the center has proved less than vital and the left is too often indistinguishable from the center. There will always be need for areas of compromise within our political system. No liberal party—and no conservative party—can hope to impose a doctrinaire will without some appreciation of both the variables and vagaries of our complex national and local life. But in recent years "compromise" has become almost an end in itself, and it is the liberal who is deemed extremist when he voices any strength of conviction; the result, in fact, is not "compromise," but stalemate, not the achievement of the possible but the enthronement of the status quo, not moderation but immobility, not the clear delineation of public issues but a spreading sense that there are no longer any important public questions on which men may reasonably be asked to give more than equivocal answers. There is no shortage of great themes for political combat, but rather a loss of nerve among most of our political warriors. It is time for a new beginning.

PART II

ISSUES

CHAPTER 5

The Time of the Bomb:

Notes on

Adult Delinquency

IN A TELEVISION INTERVIEW with Edward R. Murrow in February, 1958, Harry Truman aggressively disclaimed any moral torment or irresolution about the use of the atomic bomb on Hiroshima. "When we had this powerful new weapon," he said, "I had no qualms about using it because a weapon of war is a destructive weapon." Mr. Truman proceeded to emphasize that he yielded to no man in his distaste for war, but he could see no special complexity about the introduction of the A-bomb. It was, so to speak, all in the hard day's work of the Presidency; moreover, he said, mankind could be confident that "if the world gets into turmoil," the H-bomb would be employed just as the A-bomb had been. "You can be sure of that," he added.

In putting the matter this way, Mr. Truman may have been—as he so often is—unfair to himself; his capacity for verbal parody of his own deeds is often limitless. Certainly the archives suggest that the dropping of the bomb was neither a capricious nor routine exercise, and that moral considerations were not excluded from the reflections of many of the men associated with the project.

In a sense, nevertheless, Mr. Truman's statement joins the issue for many of us. The physical consequences of the bomb-throwing are matters of record: 64,000 dead at once, many more thousands injured; the casualty list is still incomplete nearly fifteen years later. We have by now grown accustomed to reading such figures without flinching. There is nothing very new about that; man has always shown a remarkable talent for adjusting to mass horror while turning away from the sight of a solitary marred face.

What gives Mr. Truman's comment a singular place in history is that it seems to mark a crucial stage in man's acceptance of an age of madness. (In November, 1959, in opposition to the views of Stevenson, Humphrey and Kennedy, Mr. Truman was noisily clamoring for unilateral resumption of nuclear tests, as if to affirm his obliviousness to the moral crisis created by the atomic age.)

It is not simply because the decision to bring hell to Hiroshima was made that one quarrels with Mr. Truman; I know all the arguments—that speedy termination of the war saved thousands of lives, Japanese and American alike, and that no one can truly estimate what the final price of prolonged hostilities on the mainland might have been. Given the intolerable nature of the choice, let no one claim any retroactive wisdom. What cannot be so charitably viewed is the state of mind that enables a man to insist that the decision was easy, simple, never in doubt.

This is not a particular comment on Harry Truman, by all accounts a generous and kindly man forever getting into trouble because of his warm concern for old cronies, but a comment on the human condition induced by the long series of blows administered to the processes of reason in the twentieth century. Only in a punch-drunk civilization could Mr. Truman have spoken such words so carelessly and have done so without evoking any noticeable outcry of public pain. For the simple-minded, columnist George Sokolsky summed things up this way:

"The Russians like to threaten. They never stop threatening us over Berlin and yet they know that nothing could do them as much damage as a war. Granted that a war would hurt us just as much and perhaps even more, no matter what happens to us, all the newly built establishments of Soviet industrialism would undoubtedly be wiped out during the first few days of a nuclear war . . . What then would become of Soviet Russia? The cynical will ask, what will become of the United States, but that is not here the issue."

End of debate.

That is the mood and style governing much of the discussion over modern weapons. I know it will be said that, after all, there was only a quantitative difference between Hiroshima and the Nazi bombings of Rotterdam, Coventry and so many other places, and the counterterror ultimately inflicted on Berlin, Frankfurt and other great German citadels, where air raids were equally undiscriminating in their choice of victims. Hiroshima was merely the climax of a process begun when man accepted the notion that war was too big a sport to be confined to the combatant troops and decided to let women and children into the game. There are even those who intimate it is symptomatic of a "softness" on Communism that so many men in the West look with anguish at a form of aerial bombardment only more effective in degree than that employed against the Nazis.

The argument may give us pause but not, I trust, for too long. From 1914 till the present man has been steadily engaged in perfecting instruments for his own destruction, and World War II was his climactic rehearsal for doomsday. Must the show go on simply because so much has been invested in the tryouts? To look at it another way, we were lucky to get out of the last holocaust alive—and a lot of people didn't. We are now on notice. Are we too far gone to read the signs?

I am alternately fascinated and appalled when I see ordinarily gentle, soft-spoken people suddenly achieve the hard look of military strategists as they calmly weigh the gamesmanship involved in the modern diplomatic jousting that can only be described as blind man's bluff. I profess no expertness in military matters; my private war with a rifle on the playing fields of Camp Lee has been recounted in an earlier book; and when the parlor discussion turns to the possibilities inherent in the anti-anti-missile-missile, I am out of it. But such ignorance no longer disqualifies me from the discussion. For all that I have to know—and on this point the military scholars appear to be in quite general agreement—is that the potential for mutual annihilation now exists, and that the concept of "victory" in war has become obsolete. By the same token the phrase "calculated risk" has lost all its traditional meaning.

I am aware of the argument that, given certain advances in intercontinental ballistic missiles plus certain optimum conditions for the supreme adventure plus a certain languor in high places, a day can be visualized on which even so vast a nation as ours might be smitten with a blow so paralyzing that "massive retaliation" would be impossible. It would be the perfect international crime; it would make Pearl Harbor seem like pretty small stuff. This is the nightmare periodically held before us when anyone dares to question the military obsession or to urge priorities for any endeavors other than military defense.

Since I am committed to the proposition that almost anything is possible (in the year 1959, for example, the Yankees finished fourth), I do not exclude this implausibility, nor do I write of it lightly. I should hardly propose that all our researches be halted and that we serenely embrace the notion that the "balance of terror" detected by Winston Churchill is immutable. Indeed, given the existing circumstances, there is clearly no escape from some preoccupation with Moloch's matters.

Nevertheless I ask that there be long moments set aside for contemplation of the spectacle of which we as a nation are now a part, and in which so much of mankind occupies the role of innocent bystander. I submit that if we could but see ourselves in the human drama as we might be seen from the moon or some of the other domains to which we are currently reaching, both the sadness and ridiculousness of our posture might produce an awakening. Perhaps we might even understand why some of the younger set fail to take us seriously and decline to exhibit a healthy interest in civics and community welfare projects.

Here we are, distraught and disorganized on the one hand by juvenile delinquency in our midst, forming committees, councils and cabals to control the hoodlums, beseeching a little respect for law and order, debating whether a "big stick" or larger psychiatric facilities contain the answer to trouble in the streets, asking ourselves what has happened to the values that ought to inspire the respect of these violent characters. And here we are poised continuously on the edge of a big blowup, telling ourselves that this state of things must continue indefinitely and that only the faint-hearted cry havoc and that it is a test of national character and nerve for us to live this way and like it, and that if the worst comes to the worst, better that more of us survive than they, and so on into the long night. Let us be vigilant in barring the sale of switch blades, but let no one remove our atomic toys.

I have succumbed to no illusions about the eagerness of the Russian leaders to negotiate great and lasting settlements of all our discords. Nor do I have to be reminded that they have often behaved as if agreements are to be reached only to be breached. What I do contest is the view that any attempt to end or curb the arms race is doomed before it begins because of the intrinsic nature of Muscovite mischievousness.

There are times when one detects hints that the Communist leaders have revised their own gospel in deference to the qualitative changes in warfare wrought by the atomic era. It was their classic thesis that "wars and revolutions" were the inevitable manifestations of the chronic ailments of decaying capitalist society; unpleasant as the shooting might be, it must finally produce dividends for their side; heads they win, tails we lose.

But the H-bomb has changed all that. No commissar can say with conviction that his dream world will rise from the ashes of atomic conflict; the remnants of man that might survive such a struggle would hardly constitute much of a prize for the victor; the mastery of wasteland is a dubious vision.

Not long ago the *Paris-Presse* published what purported to be an account of a conversation that took place between H. G. Wells and V. I. Lenin back in 1920 which curiously corroborates the view that something new may be afoot. In that interview Lenin is reported to have said:

"I, too, understand that all human conceptions are on the scale of our planet. They are based on the assumption that technical potentials, when developed to the full, will not go beyond 'terrestrial limits.' If we arrive at establishing interplanetary communications we must revise all our philosophical, social and moral conceptions. In that case the technical potentials, having become unlimited, will impose upon us the end of violence as a means and method of progress."

One has no way of knowing whether Mr. Khrushchev is familiar with this remark, or whether he has fumbled toward the same conclusion independently. In the aftermath of his strange pilgrimage to America, many imponderables of Russian behavior remain as large as they ever were. But it is no real contribution merely to keep repeating that the Soviet aim is "world conquest." The fanatic drive of the Russian leaders is apparent; their allegiance to the mythology of Marxism is incontestable; their contempt for basic individual values is unmodified. But the important question is whether they have chosen to wage their war with primarily political and economic weapons, recognizing that the day of the atomic blitzkrieg is probably past because, in General Gavin's phrase, no man can tell which way the wind will blow after the air is poisoned.

In that context there should have been nothing too mystifying about the long Russian clamor for cessation of nuclear tests. For the same reason it is conceivable that progress can be made in the realm of nuclear disarmament without any fundamental resolution of the issues that divide East and West. We would in effect be agreeing to live unhappily ever after because that condition is preferable to mutual extermination. The battle would continue on the ideological and economic fronts, terrain we have often found difficult and treacherous because of our national confusion as to whether we are seeking to persuade the world of the blessings of free institutions or whether we are crusading for the special economic doctrines of the National Association of Manufacturers. Surely the prospect of even prolonged rivalry on these elusive battlegrounds should be more attractive than a condition in which a single miscalculation by fallible men can return man to the cave.

This is a form of rivalry we ought to welcome. If, for example, it means flourishing competition for the allegiance of the have-nots of the world, the dividends for humanity might be considerable. And if the conflict obliges us to examine even more carefully the imperfections of our free institutions, that, too, must be regarded as a general gain.

So the prospect of prolonged dispute on these levels ought to be inspiring rather than depressing. But it is premised on the avoidance of an accidental encounter from which there might be no turning back and in which all the weapons of annihilation might be employed on a moment's notice —a kind of mutual suicide pact instantly executed.

Dean Acheson has revealed there was a day during the Korean war when the nation's leaders were informed by the Pentagon that a Russian air attack on the U.S. was under way. Some poor fellow had misread the atmospheric signs; the Air Force was alerted at once. Mr. Acheson did not spell out the details by which the error was discovered in time; but the outline of the story is enough to suggest that we are all actors in a true cliff-hanger, and that too few of us realize exactly how dangerously we are living.

I will be told that great advances have been made in reducing the margin of error and that a future mistake of this dimension is almost unthinkable. But the key word is "almost"; for we have now reached the point at which neither team is permitted the luxury of more than one mistake. We are playing under new rules: a "sudden death" period is at hand, with one fumble ending the ball game, and neither captain likely to be around to claim the ball.

There are some optimistic fellows who see a unique virtue in the nuclear period. It is their view that the existence of the Big Bombs has actually ushered in a new age of compulsory peace; The Thing has dictated the terms of a great tacit nonaggression agreement because no nation dares to invite the risk of the final explosion. Remove the threat, they contend, and this great restraint is banished. Blessed are the bomb-makers; they are saving man from himself.

The trouble with this tranquilizer is that it again rejects the element of accident in history. I am not referring solely to the kind of man-failure cited by Acheson, but to the misreading of an enemy's designs and intentions that is a continuous hazard in the game of brinkmanship. Bluff, bluster and blackmail have achieved a new dimension in the time of The Bomb; for there remains the peril of that moment when the Russians must weigh how far they can press their offensive, and once the guessing game begins, we are all headed toward the point of no return, even though neither side desires the ultimate collision.

I am assuming that the concept of "preventive war" is discredited, in Washington and Moscow alike. The lurking sense of national guilt that Hiroshima has left with us— regardless of the strategic merits of the awful argument— makes it inconceivable that any American leadership would seriously contemplate this course. While we can speak with less authority about a regime which displays no visible reverence for individual human life and has on occasion found easy justification for large slaughter, it must also be said that we have no evidence of total lunacy in the Kremlin. The indications, as suggested earlier, are rather that the contemporary Communists are disposed to conduct their major operations through political intrigue and economic beguilement. But the threat of atomic war remains a weapon of diplomacy—for both sides. As long as it does, the possibility of error cannot be discounted. How do the Communists *know* what we would do if Peking undertook a frontal assault on Formosa? Do we *know* what we would do? Would the U.S. countenance another Korean war of attrition, or would the pressure for "getting it over with" become irresistible? Out of such imponderables great international confusions are born. It has proved difficult enough to conduct national dialogues with the commissars. If we find conversation so hard, if we so often feel that we speak different languages on every level, can we be confident that we correctly read each other's minds?

If we could banish The Bomb overnight and pretend the monster had never been conceived, our problems would hardly be at an end; from a certain viewpoint, as previously acknowledged, the dangers of collision might be greater. Nor am I maintaining that there was anything idyllic about the conventional type of World War I warfare in which, Cyril Falls has estimated, 12,000,000 soldiers perished before the shooting ceased.* It is, in fact, against the wretched record of our century—two world wars and a succession of smaller ones—that I urge examination of the preposterousness of the modern predicament. And what I challenge here is not the notion that things are tough and complicated, but the habit of mind which almost matter-of-factly speculates about the shape of military marvels to come.

* *The Great War* (New York, G. P. Putnam's Sons, 1959).

Conceivably we are all doomed; there are those who think we deserve to be after what we have done to blight the promise of this century and to convert the miracles of science into a chamber of horrors. I choose not to submit quietly or, as others have done, to confuse our seeming helplessness with national virtue. I can recite all the crimes in the Russian book; one need hardly go further back than the ruthless suppression of the Hungarian revolution to glimpse the nature of the system which has devoured its own children and a lot of other peoples' too. But when the catalogue is complete, there remains the larger failure common to all of us—that we have let things reach a point at which we cannot even speak with confidence about the prospect of human survival.

Perhaps there is no turning back even now; nothing guarantees a happy ending to our story. I urge only that we see the idiocy into which we have converted the human comedy: the picture of busy little men feverishly building and planning and scheming and inventing and dreaming and revising the super-colossal deathtrap which is the last scene of the last act.

Let us paint the picture, and hang it where all men can see it; and perhaps before it is too late there can be a universal dawning. Possibly the sight will interrupt crass politics-as-usual, and even give rise to new ideas about how we can extricate ourselves from the dead end into which we have all been maneuvered.

The alternative is to continue through the same mad motions, serene in the righteousness of our cause and looking forward to some other-worldly reward once we have endured hell on earth.

I repeat: given a great new effort, a new vision of the idiocy of our present state, there are no assurances of success. The answers are not in the back of this or any book. But at least we may reassert our dignity as human beings and, if it is to the cave that we are headed, let it be recorded that we used every resource of human intelligence in trying to avert that result.

No great nation, it is said in the ancient cliché, can survive if it is unprepared to fight for its life. No American Legion convention could be complete without the embodiment of that sentiment in resolution form. I am sufficiently reconciled to what are known as the harsh realities to despair of any salvation through unilateral disarmament.

But I also despair of the men who have reconciled themselves to the inevitability of atomic war—or who, at best, believe that only an ever-growing atomic arsenal can save us from a fate worse than death.

Moreover, above and beyond all the strategic calculations lies the moral one; yet not until the latter months of 1959 did a major voice outside the orthodox pacifist ranks dare to raise it bluntly. Then it was that George Kennan appealed to the country to re-examine the policy of nuclear deterrence on "a straight issue of conscience."

He voiced personal horror that any great free nation should rest its hope for security on the prospective use of weapons which would "destroy innocent noncombatant human life, including the lives of children, on a vast scale." How, he asked, could we be confident of the righteousness of a cause based on this strategy of total horror—on a "hideous self-centeredness . . . an irresponsibility toward the continuity of life which has no foundation in the Judaic-Christian tradition?" It was not the first time that Kennan had been ahead of his time in calling for re-examination of accepted postures, and once again the amount of thought and concern he stirred indicated how unsatisfied most Americans were with the banal prescriptions of the cold warriors.

Kennan's position was that we were committed to a concept of defense at variance with all our best instincts. He was advocating neither retreat nor surrender, but rather a sober review of the notion that atomic arms should be our shield. Beyond that he was saying that there is a moral brink at which a free nation must pause.

I despair, too, of those who have grown obsessed with the business of creating a vast network of underground shelters to which we can presumably retire in orderly procession if our adversaries have the grace to give us adequate warning and avoid dropping any lethal stuff in our friendly neighborhood.

I despair of those who feel a certain relaxation after it has been reported that ninety-seven percent of the sirens employed in an air-raid drill functioned with magnificent clarity and precision.

I despair of those who call for negotiations from "positions of strength" but somehow manage to scorn negotiations until our very position of strength may have been dissipated.

I despair of those who cry out in one breath that it is damnable immorality to negotiate with bloodstained despots and clamor shortly thereafter for new economic aid for Franco Spain.

There is an inescapable immorality in shaking hands and posing for the TV cameras with the men whose guns and tanks crushed the Hungarian revolt (to say nothing of what they have done to large numbers of their own people guilty of lesser heresies than insurrection). But I submit there is an infinitely vaster immorality in passively accepting—even preparing for—an atomic free-for-all from which not the smallest child nor the oldest woman will have the faintest hope of immunity.

A recent Congressional inquiry estimated that a surprise nuclear attack would bring death to 50,000,000 Americans and serious injury to 20,000,000 more.

A special Task Force appointed by Governor Rockefeller reported at about the same time that the creation of a bomb-shelter system, including inexpensive do-it-yourself units, could appreciably reduce the toll of radiation victims under certain conditions—such as the limited duration of attack—which might, of course, not be conveniently fulfilled.

I concede the obligation of the chief executive of a state to think of everything, including the worst; he might even be deemed delinquent in his duties if he did not consider the possibility that such an assault could occur. While one may say that life would hardly seem worth living in the ruins of an atomic disaster, presumably that is a matter for the survivors to decide; it may be that a number of those who were still around would be grateful for the Governor's prescience.

The efficacy of the whole shelter program is open to long technical dispute, but I have no particular quarrel with the view that the endeavor is worth considering even if, when the dark day comes, it might result only in the reduction of the national death toll to 37,643,512. Certainly a case, however macabre, can be made for the position that this leaves a lot of people, perhaps enough to start all over again the pursuit of sanity. The issue is not whether such a program should be considered; it is a matter of the priority assigned to it, and the spirit in which it is undertaken.

If it is seen as the desperate resort of a civilization with its back to the wall, as a last exercise in life-saving to be employed when nearly all that is of consequence is lost, there is nothing wholly objectionable about it.

But if it is presented as the "answer" to the finality of atomic disaster, if it is offered as reassurance to those who are appalled by the hazards of brinkmanship, if it is deemed a device for strengthening our national nerve and resolution in confronting a rough adversary, if it is accompanied—as in the case of Governor Rockefeller—by a call for renewal of atomic tests, then it is another symptom of the decline of our senses and the hardening of all our intellectual arteries.

Unfortunately, that is exactly how it is being presented. In proclaiming his support for the Rockefeller shelter plan, Allen Dulles, Director of the Central Intelligence Agency, said "the evidence is overwhelming that the Soviets intend to use nuclear blackmail as a major weapon to promote their objectives—namely, to spread communism throughout the world." This was the theory propounded by the Rockefeller Task Force.

With half of the proposition there can be little dispute; undoubtedly the Russians do use the specter of atomic annihilation as a diplomatic club and, in countermeasure, so do we. But does anyone seriously maintain that the emergence of a network of shelters would drastically transform our attitude toward the prospect of atomic conflict? Is it asserted that we could be bolder and colder at the bargaining table if we knew that the national casualty list might—again assuming the dubious perfectibility of shelter structures—be reduced from 70,000,000 to 45,000,000?

Clearly this is absurdity. It is characteristic, however, of much of the strategic hocus-pocus of an age in which multiple atrocity has created a numbness in high places. We have almost lost the capacity to see ourselves as history may see us, if there are any places from which the view is unobstructed. While we may still wince at the traffic fatalities of a holiday week end, we can hold solemn public conclaves at which the arithmetic of atomic death is discussed as coolly as if we were talking about the incidence of chicken pox among children. And the editorial writer on the *Daily News* can intermittently thunder his uninhibited warnings to the enemy: Let them make one false move and we'll give it to them in atomic spades.

Who dares challenge such bravado?

"One effect of the First World War was to make it impossible for me to go on living in a world of abstractions," Bertrand Russell has written.

"I used to watch young men embarking in troop trains to be slaughtered on the Somme because generals were stupid. I felt an aching compassion for these young men, and found myself united to the actual world in a strange marriage of pain.

"All the high-flown thoughts that I had about the abstract world of ideas seemed to me thin and rather trivial in view of the vast suffering that surrounded me. The nonhuman world remained as an occasional refuge, but not as a country in which to build one's permanent home."

The reaffirmation of such a sentiment in our day would be considered in many quarters as a manifestation of "softness," an inexcusable intimation that we may be losing our appetite for the great engagement, a sign of weakness sure to be exploited by the cunning commissars. To resist "blackmail" we must demonstrate that we are not scared, and to prove we are not scared we must build the best damn bomb shelters ever erected anywhere.

Ah, but I can hear the investigating Senator asking, would it be a matter of indifference to you who won if the terrible conflict ever began? If one can visualize victory, of course it would not be; and if I am asked whether I would prefer enslavement to death, I hope I can say truthfully that I stand with Patrick Henry.

My plea is against those who would tell us these intolerable alternatives are all that are left to us; that there are no margins left for maneuver; that we are living on borrowed time anyway.

I have said there are no easy formulae for achieving even the turbulent form of competitive survival that may be the best hope of the immediate future. But I am disturbed by the prevalence of the notion that there is something dishonorable or craven about the continuance of the quest. In the years immediately following World War II there was the unmistakable danger of quick Russian thrusts against a demobilized, war-weary West; the coup in Czechoslovakia symbolized the peril. In that period it seemed clear that only creation of "positions of strength" could prevent the disintegration of the front of freedom. I thought the Communist-sponsored Third Party movement of 1948 contained the potential of real peril because, had it achieved any major demonstration of public support, it might well have tempted the Russians into larger adventures based on the premise that we had withdrawn from the world.

But to build "positions of strength" and simultaneously sponsor the economic revival of Western Europe through the Marshall Plan was a vital holding operation, not a blueprint for all time. It was designed to set the stage for negotiation among equals, not to usher in an endless arms race.

What has happened, however, is that the desperate expediencies of those years have been rationalized into the long-range policy of influential men in the Pentagon, the Atomic Energy Commission and some other strategic areas of government. That is why it is so difficult, among other things, to ascertain the exact truth about some negotiations that have occurred in the realm of disarmament. That is why the Voice of America has so often seemed to have the quality of double-think. That is why Mr. Eisenhower's instinctive desire to serve as mediator among men has so often been blunted and obscured by those committed to the doctrine that even limited agreements are either impossible or dangerous.

This is written shortly after Mr. Nixon's mission to Moscow and Mr. Khrushchev's journey to America, and at a time when modest hope has momentarily acquired respectability. Such episodes serve to emphasize the duality which has clouded our national attitudes throughout the Eisenhower years. One shudders to think of what Mr. Nixon might have said about a Democratic President who proposed to send his Vice-President on a junket to Moscow, even with all its argumentative adornments; for if this trip had any serious meaning, it was as an exploratory voyage preliminary to more extensive dialogue.

But contrast these events with the response accorded Adlai Stevenson in October, 1956, when he pledged that his first act as president would be to seek world agreement for the banning of H-bomb tests.

"We are caught up today, along with the rest of the world, in an arms race that threatens mankind with stark, merciless, bleak catastrophe," he said.

"The search for peace will not end, it will begin with the halting of these tests. What we will accomplish is a new beginning and the world needs nothing so much as a new beginning."

Stevenson's plea was swiftly brushed aside by the President.

Indeed, at one juncture Mr. Eisenhower declared that he had spoken his "last word" on the subject and declined to answer further questions. As in many episodes, the President was to modify his stand before the end of his term; a one-year suspension of tests was announced on October 31, 1958; in effect the essence of Stevenson's proposal was accepted. But by August 12, 1959, a UPI dispatch was reporting:

WASHINGTON—The Administration is wrestling with the problem of whether to resume nuclear weapons tests this fall. This was made known today by key officials as pressure built up for a resumption of high altitude and small weapons tests.

The atom warriors die hard.

Perhaps it should be added that Stevenson's proposal stirred some consternation and resistance among some of the Democratic "pros" as well as in the White House inner circle. To many of the "pros" it was another symptom of his incorrigible eggheadedness. In fact it was a call for a consistent American image:

"This is one matter on which the defeatist view that nothing can be done must be broken. I say that something can be done; that the deadlock can be broken; that the world can make a new beginning toward peace.

"And, finally, I say that America should take the initiative; that it will reassure millions of people all around the globe who are troubled by our reliance on nuclear weapons, our concepts of massive retaliation, if mighty, magnanimous America spoke up for the rescue of man from the elemental fire which we have kindled."

The tests went on for two more years; each time that sober scientific voices suggested we might be engaged in a massive long-range plan to poison ourselves, there were tough-minded men ready to produce statistics showing that fallout wasn't nearly as harmful as the pessimists asserted. At times we seemed determined to prove that modern man could achieve the miracle of becoming a little bit pregnant and staying that way.

And from the moment the one-year moratorium took effect, the crusade for resumption of the tests was on. Some men just couldn't get enough of the stuff. There were some days of the week when the President tried to say to the world that it was time men stopped thinking about victory in an H-bomb war; there could only be vanquished. But there were other days of the week when his Secretary of Defense could not resist proclaiming that we were invincible, and begging for the chance to show off his atomic arsenal to Russian visitors.

With unusual tenacity the President clung to the notion in 1959 that something could be done. He appeared to be genuinely exerting himself in behalf of disarmament moves; in his demeanor and tone one recognized the man who had said some months earlier that the universal yearning for peace was so deep that "governments better get out of the way." But it was easier to respect his instincts than to discern his mastery of events. Even as the Geneva talks seeking renewal of the atomic-test ban were in progress, Atomic Energy Commissioner John A. McCone was urging that the accord be resumed on no more than a "week-to-week" basis unless the Russians fully accepted our terms. Clearly the Administration, like the political world, was still deeply divided between those who felt an awful immediacy about the peril in which mankind found itself and those who viewed the strategic problems of the atomic age as essentially no different from any other, and war itself as a tolerable recourse if something went wrong with gamesmanship.

So we stumble and drift, torn between a vague awareness that we are on the edge of no man's land and the self-righteous certitude that everything will turn out all right if we talk loftily and carry a big stick. And teen-agers are admonished to drive carefully.

CHAPTER 6

Men and Government

BACK IN the month of May of the year 1956 the complicated life of White House Press Secretary James Hagerty was beset by new exasperation. The plague of foot-in-mouth disease had stricken a high if heretofore obscure Administration official, one Howard Pyle, deputy assistant to the President.

The unfortunate Mr. Pyle had chosen that month of all months for a journey to Detroit. It was a time of gloom and bitterness in the capital and provinces of the auto industry. Michigan's unemployment rolls had reached 190,000; Detroit's Welfare Department reported a 400-percent rise in relief applications in four weeks; many still listed as employed were actually working only three days a week. In the official language, Detroit was a "critical job area" and things seemed to be getting worse rather than better.

At that unpropitious moment Mr. Pyle met with reporters in his Detroit hotel room and delivered this comment: "The right to suffer is one of the joys of a free economy, just as the right to prosper is. But Michigan will come out of it, just as the farmers are doing now."

For nearly twenty-four hours the wire services inexplicably

neglected to transmit Mr. Pyle's remarks, which had received moderate but prompt attention in the Detroit *Times*. Not until UAW President Walter Reuther released a telegram of protest to the President did the press associations let the rest of the country share Detroit's secret.*

The news traveled slowly, but it got around. And since it is not a very long time from May to November, especially in an election year, there was consternation in Mr. Hagerty's office. Mr. Pyle had blundered, and he soon felt obliged to issue a statement of clarification: "The hardships of unemployment any time, anywhere are not pleasant for any of us, but to date the most dedicated efforts of all concerned, including Mr. Reuther, have not been able to prevent them completely." In short, Mr. Pyle wished he had known when to remain quiet.

The episode must have been a peculiarly shattering one for Mr. Hagerty's ministry of propaganda because it occurred less than two years after a comparable gaucherie by Defense Secretary Charles E. Wilson. At a news conference—in Detroit as well—on October 11, 1954, Mr. Wilson had rendered a philosophical observation of his own about unemployment. He preferred a bird dog to a kennel dog, he said, because "he will go out and hunt for food rather than sit on his fanny and yell." The timing of Mr. Wilson's indiscretion must have been even more irksome to Mr. Hagerty because less than a month remained before the Congressional elections. So the blunt-spoken Mr. Wilson soon found himself lamenting his "unfortunate mistake" and apologizing for his "inept remarks" and extending to their excellencies, the unemployed, assurances of his highest concern.

---

* And not for more than forty-eight hours after the incident occurred did the N. Y. *Daily News,* the N. Y. *Daily Mirror* or the N. Y. *Journal-American* carry any reference to the episode.

Yet perhaps such episodes were placed in their truest perspective by Mr. Pyle a week after his own retraction. With renewed disregard for Mr. Hagerty's jangled sensitivities, he announced during a jaunt to Phoenix that the President had at no time chastised him for his political blunder. "It might interest you to know," he told reporters, "that the President and I have never even discussed it."

The agonies to which Mr. Hagerty has been subjected by such loose talk are less important than the glimpses these incidents offer of some minds in motion. I am sure Mr. Wilson has no special partisanship for bird dogs over people; he seems an affable man; I am also sure that on reflection Mr. Pyle did not mean to propose a national "strength-through-joy-of-suffering" movement. What both men were saying, it seems to me, is that the fate of the unemployed is not a proper primary concern of government and that, perhaps incidentally, a little bit of joblessness provides an atmosphere most likely to insure the survival of the fittest. The callousness of the imagery they employed merely dramatizes the central economic argument that will confront us if we manage to avoid an international explosion. The issue is whether a society as large and complicated as ours can achieve any long-range sense and perform any positive function in the world without an infinitely larger degree of national planning than we have seriously contemplated so far.

This is not merely an argument of sentiment, but neither do I exclude that factor. Those who literally do not give a damn about the human suffering involved in cyclical unemployment; those who can say honestly that they are unmoved by the reminder that more than half the world's populace goes to bed hungry each night; those who are quite persuaded that the plight of a Bowery derelict or an Asian peasant is his own responsibility and has no meaning for the lives of the rest of us; those who believe that, under the mystic laws of what is loosely called the "free-enterprise system," thrift, industry and virtue are almost invariably rewarded while sloth and extravagance are punished—those, in sum, who believe this is the best of all economic worlds and Adam Smith the voice of the deity, will find little to cheer here. Neither will there be much area of accord with those who deem a balanced budget—and lower taxes—the only cause worth fighting for amid world-wide hunger and disease.

I began with unemployment because the recurrence of large-scale economic exile—in those intervals we describe as "recessions"—has become so accepted a fact of modern life; and this acceptance seems to me both irrational and immoral. There are, of course, certain industrialists—fewer this decade than two decades ago, I trust—who regard a "modest" level of joblessness as a plain good thing; it "keeps the people who have jobs on their toes"; it may even dilute the militancy of unions. I have no talent for addressing myself to men who would seem to be boasting that their hearts are as hard as their heads.

But there are others who still quite seriously believe that government is the true enemy. The notion that the intervention of the state in economic affairs may ultimately make robots of us all is an old and specious cry. As long as basic liberties of speech and assemblage are protected, there is no reason to dread the effective uses of government power. Now, as in the early days of the New Deal, it is simply the bogeyman of those who really mean that business should have its own way.

Whenever it is suggested that we are doomed to "regimentation" if we permit any real degree of government planning, I am reminded of a story of the 1930's. It was about the suburban commuter who rose each day at exactly

6:40 A.M., who breakfasted each day at exactly 7:05 A.M., who left his home each day at exactly 7:25 A.M. to catch the 7:52 A.M. train. He served dutifully at his bank post, arriving at exactly 9 A.M., lunching between exactly noon and 1 P.M. on exactly the same fare at the same restaurant, and at exactly 5 P.M. he left the bank to catch the 5:20 P.M. And on the train homeward he would approvingly read an editorial in the old New York *Sun* and exclaim to his train companion:

"By God, we've got to be careful or that man Roosevelt will regiment us."

The poor fellow may still be keeping the same schedule and seeing the same peril. But he is, after all, only the Caspar Milquetoast of a larger joke in which business and agricultural interests—and their mouthpieces in the press—decry all forms of "paternalism" except those favorable to their own private welfare.

Unhappily few of those journals which decry federal subsidy of public works are equally dedicated in their opposition to federal subsidy of their postal rates; the same paradox could be cited in many areas. Nevertheless, despite all the contradictions and ironies, the mystique of laissez faire still dominates much of the language of public debate.

Thus it is that there is virtually no semblance of national planning to avert unemployment and, when the deluge comes, there is great and bipartisan resistance to any federal program for doing something about it.

One year after the 1929 economic collapse, Herbert Hoover was intoning:

"This is not an issue as to whether people shall go hungry or cold in the United States. It is solely a question of the best method by which hunger and cold can be prevented. It is a question as to whether the American people on the one hand will maintain the spirit of charity and mutual self-help through voluntary giving and the responsibility of local government as distinguished on the other hand from the appropriations out of the Federal treasury for such purposes. My own conviction is strongly that if we break down this sense of responsibility of individual generosity to individual and mutual self-help in the country in times of national difficulty and if we start appropriations of this character we have not only impaired something infinitely valuable in the life of the American people but have struck at the roots of self-government."

We are not the same land today; we have some built-in protections against the initial impact of joblessness; recessions do not automatically mean bread lines and apple-selling. Neither, however, is there any justification for the prevalent view that unemployment has virtually ceased to matter in our society, and that human damage wrought by these cyclical disturbances is unworthy of general concern.

Six months after Black Friday of 1929, Karl Schriftgeisser recalls in *This Was Normalcy*, the Hoover Administration estimated unemployment at 3,187,000; six months later the figure was set at 4,000,000. Then, as now, the accuracy of the statistics was challenged by economists and labor leaders who accused the government press agents of calculated underestimation. The interesting thing is that, when unemployment in the latest Eisenhower recession fell just below 3,500,000, there were great hosannahs emanating from Washington and Republican spokesmen offered the figures as proof that the President's studied inaction had been an act of master statesmanship. Of course the comparative figures must also be weighed, in an economic sense, against the vast expansion of the labor force; we are now talking of an economy in which more than 60,000,000 are employed (oh, wild dream of Henry Wallace and all the eggheads of the early forties) as against 47,900,000 in 1929. Contrasting the percentage has large bearing on the seriousness of the economic trouble. But it in no way reduces the grievous human trouble which we are prepared to countenance in the name of conservative economic shibboleth.

Even as we were emerging from recession in 1959, there were prophecies of new "inevitabilities." William F. Butler, vice president of the Chase Manhattan Bank, was quoted in November of that year as warning that "there is a prospect of another recession in 1961." Despite the "many sweeping changes in our economic affairs in the past few decades, the business cycle has not been repealed," Butler observed with finality.

Amid all our wealth and untapped resources, must we still proclaim to the world that we are recurrently the helpless creatures of a plague called the "business cycle"?

The cruel and inhuman punishment to which men, women and children are periodically subjected by both cyclical and seasonal unemployment will hardly move those who have comfortably told themselves there is always work for the industrious. A considerable portion of our press still finds more satisfaction in exposing a random relief "chiseler" than in describing the frustrations and indignity which decent people suffer on relief. The New York *Daily News*, whose editorial page in recent years has become sort of a poor man's *Wall Street Journal*, regards the granting of relief funds to unmarried mothers as the large local evil of our time, and intermittently turns its full fury on such exhibitions of lawless fertility.

Any newspaperman who has covered any phase of the unemployment story knows that the vast proportion of those out of work are victims of economic circumstances far beyond their control, and derive no spiritual satisfaction from their condition. They endure a deepening degradation rendered even more acute by the knowledge that they are "special cases" in a society of mounting employment.

But throughout the long months of the latest recession the President and his advisors bitterly resisted any legislative measures designed to reduce unemployment; the Democratic Congressional leadership was almost equally lethargic, and it was considered a major move when Senate Democratic Leader Johnson finally proposed a Congressional investigation of the unemployment problem.

"Planning" and "spending" remained the dirty words of the day. Outside the ranks of labor, only a few voices, most notably that of Senator Paul Douglas, were raised to support the proposition that the periodical ills of the unemployed were relevant to the health of our national economy, and a serious moral burden.

No extraordinary ingenuity is required to visualize the kind of planning that could combat the recurrence of large-scale joblessness. Surely it would be possible to authorize a public works fund for discretionary use in the event of declining employment; such a fund, of course, would be meaningful only if the White House were inhabited by a Chief Executive who did not view spending as the basic sin, and who was less disposed to believe in the doctrine of business infallibility.

I should hardly maintain that this is the only answer, or necessarily the most desirable one. There remains the whole problem of far-reaching legislation to aid "depressed areas." Beyond that lie all the neglected or discarded plans for concerted national economic growth, resting now in a variety of pigeonholes and likely to be brought forth only for brief campaign use during the autumn of 1960.

Others may offer wiser programs. My contention here is only that, three decades after the departure of Mr. Hoover, some of the myths which paralyzed his Administration in a time of national panic still plague us. The belief that there is some fatal conflict between freedom and government—rather than between free government and despotism—still guides a large number of the nation's editorial pages, and inhibits the leaders of both major parties. Nothing has more deeply roused Messrs. Johnson and Rayburn in recent months than the President's intimation that they were profligates; they became consumed with a determination to prove that they were the truly parsimonious ones.

Their conduct led the Washington *Post and Times Herald* to comment after the recess of Congress in the autumn of 1959 and the sharp exchanges between Mr. Eisenhower and the Democratic Congressional leadership:

". . . Instead of contesting his [the President's] basic assumption, spokesmen for the majority have replied meekly that the Democrats weren't as bad as he said they were. This reaction illustrates very clearly, we think, why the large issues of public need have received such scant attention. Liberal Democrats and Republicans who believe that the government ought to be spending (and collecting) more for such programs as education aren't going to offset the President's negativism by seeking to outdo him."

Such basic reforms of the New Deal era as social security remain unmolested. The outlines of the welfare state will not be obliterated; they may well explain why, with all our planlessness and aimlessness, we have so far escaped any desperate economic reversal. New investment and the surge of innovation have bolstered us through the postwar years. But there is a dead-center aspect to all our economic affairs. When it is suggested that the time for a new advance is at hand, we are reminded that our standard of living is the wonder of the world, and we certainly have the gadgets to prove it. And if three to four or five million people are intermittently at a loss for work, we boast that the country has come out of the trouble fine each time it has happened in recent years.

The battle cry of do-nothingism has similarly haunted our running war with inflation. There, as in the matter of unemployment, President Eisenhower has repeatedly pictured himself as the savior of Our Way of Life by standing firmly for a course of supine inactivity. Finally, in the seventh year of his Administration, he expressed confidence that the price-wage cycle had been halted, and he cited the apparent plateau as evidence of the wisdom and virtue of nonintervention.

Whether his boast was justified remains to be seen; in any event it was a dubious triumph. Government controls—of prices, wages or anything else—have no intrinsic beauty; few men love them for their own sake, and all of us who lived through World War II are aware of the difficulties involved in applying them equitably. But fear of controls can be even more stultifying than an excessive passion for them.

Even a conservative government does not, of course, remain entirely faithful to its stereotypes when it runs into trouble. While piously avoiding any intervention in the wage-price spiral and damning such an idea as heathen doctrine, the Eisenhower Administration found no subversion in the credit-squeeze frantically imposed by the Federal Reserve Board. While proclaiming a balanced budget as the supreme goal of modern man, the Administration early in 1958 abruptly quickened the tempo of government expenditures already authorized, hastily approved other new Congressional appropriations and backed the extension of unemployment compensation—all orthodox Keynesian measures designed to

"prime the pump." In extremis, a business-minded administration does not leave everything in the hands of business
and providence. But it is likely to act ineptly, without any
real coherence, and then sit back to await the next deluge.

Certainly there were occasions during the long years of
advancing inflation when at least limited, selective controls
might well have been desirable and were at least worthy of
full public consideration. J. K. Galbraith, for example, urged
the establishment of a federal price-wage board to review
agreements in such "administered-price" industries as steel.
He argued that only such a board, empowered to review the
often collusive arrangements between corporate giants and
big unions, could protect the economy from the wage-price
merry-go-round. Such a board would, for example, be authorized to decide whether a wage agreement reached by the
contending parties could be absorbed by the industry involved without a price increase, and to block the agreement
if a price rise appeared to be dictated.

Were there flaws in this proposal? Perhaps there were.
What is noteworthy, however, is that such recommendations
were virtually excluded from the arena of general debate.
The President served notice that he regarded "peacetime
controls" as alien to our system; the editorial sages dutifully
echoed him; the politicians of both parties shrank from the
discussion, as if fearful that they would be hunted down by
David Lawrence if they were caught discussing the taboo
topic in public.

So we continued to live under what Dr. Ben W. Lewis, in
a memorable but little-noticed recital before the Monopoly
and Anti-Trust subcommittee of the Senate, has called "Economics by Admonition." This consists, he noted, of periodic
appeals by the leaders of government to the chieftains of
industry and labor "to look upon the precarious state of our

sound economy, imperiled by burgeoning inflation and yawn-
ing recession, to commune with their consciences in the vast
stillness imposed by the solemn responsibility which is theirs,
and voluntarily to restrain, even to reverse their age-old pro-
pensities and proclivities in the matter of prices and wages."

But, alas, the admonishers are destined to be ignored,
because the men to whom they address their admonitions
are not in a position to operate as society's managers. They
have enough trouble managing their own enterprises, where
the object is profit, and they cannot base their decisions on
some generalized view of the economic order. They may
quite genuinely believe that what's good for General Motors
is good for the country; but if that hypothesis is faulty, that
is Uncle Sam's misfortune. To quote Dr. Lewis:

"Consider the wage, investment and price decisions to be
made by corporate managements, and ask what contributions
consciences can make to the solution of the problems they
pose. These decisions affect all of society, not just the persons in the immediate family; and not all of those even
immediately affected can possibly be made happy by any
decisions which can possibly be made. This is quite an
assignment to impose on innocent, artless consciences. I am
not at all sure that they can stand the strain. Ponder the
plight of the management of a giant firm producing a basic
commodity, employing thousands of workers at good wages,
making splendid profits, and presently facing a crippling
strike unless it accedes to a demand for a wage increase.
The increase can easily be passed along in higher prices.
Workers want higher wages and no interruption in employment; consumers want continued output at an increasing
rate, and so do stockholders. The public does not want further inflation, and large numbers of small firms do not want
further increases in wages. The White House, which wants

high production, full employment, healthy wages, abundant profits and low prices, now admonishes industrial statesmen to recognize their public responsibility and to adopt measures "appropriate" to the maintenance of equity, full employment, stability and progress. The management—as allocator, distributor, stabilizer, trustee, conservator, prophet and chaplain, as well as manager—consults its *conscience*. The diagnosis of the attending psychiatrist will be 'multiple schizophrenia'—the management's personality will not be split, it will be shredded and powdered!"

There may come a time, as it did in the summer of 1959, when a corporate enterprise decides to draw a line and fight it out. Such a decision was apparently made by the leaders of steel. In their public manifestos they asserted that they were resisting the union's demands to save the republic from a new inflationary deluge. Yet there is reason to believe that they were motivated more by a yearning to "put the union in its place" than by any large economic altruism. In any event the Administration's long aloofness from the dispute, the President's reiteration of all the pieties about "free collective bargaining" and his reluctance even to create a fact-finding tribunal all set the stage for a prolonged struggle in which many nonparticipants suffered needless injury and in which government finally felt obliged to engage in massive punitive intervention by use of the Taft-Hartley Law.

And that didn't work, either. With the eighty-day injunction nearing its expiration, the steel workers were plainly preparing to reject the industry's "last offer" and resume their walkout. In the end Vice-President Nixon and Secretary of Labor Mitchell intervened actively and decisively; they apparently convinced the steel magnates that their cause was doomed, and they extracted a settlement more favorable to the union than the terms for which it would have settled before the long clash began. There were great hosannahs in many areas of the press for the statesmanship exhibited by Messrs. Nixon and Mitchell; few commentators paused to ask how their intervention could be reconciled with the Administration's earlier program of high-principled passivity, and what, if any, assurances they had received about the price that the steel companies would ultimately exact for this surrender.

Was there anything about this belated coup that was preferable to the early creation of a board empowered both to find facts and submit clear-cut recommendations for settlement?

It will be said by conservatives that government tribunals have always played the politics of the day, simply discovering good reasons why expedient solutions should be imposed. Their critique is a curious counterpart to the ancient Marxist conclusion that any boards of inquiry, mediation or study created by a "capitalist government" must inevitably reflect the desires of the "ruling class."

This is really a way of saying that a free society is incapable of producing a corps of learned men who adhere insofar as it is humanly possible to a body of "neutral principles" and who can reach a decision without weighing what is in it for themselves, and for their own relationships to the contending parties. I grant the difficulty involved in finding such men; we should probably have to look to the retired members of the judiciary for many of the recruits, since they are presumably men both skilled in the evaluation of conflict in claims and beyond the pressures of avarice. But it seems to me more and more clear that such

men must be found and such tribunals established if we
are to eliminate the needless waste of warfare between
increasingly powerful vested interests of both management
and labor.

I am convinced that in the steel dispute men like Dr.
George Taylor could have rendered an infinitely larger
service in the early stages of the conflict if the Eisenhower
Administration had not clung to the fetish of "nonintervention"—a spurious disguise for pro-industry partisanship.

Would our free institutions have been irreparably dam-
aged if the Galbraith plan had been in effect—if the industry
and the union had negotiated a settlement, and presented
it to a government board for review, with the object of
determining whether the increases granted would require a
price rise? It was the industry's contention that any substantial concessions would have involved a price boost, despite
the uniquely prosperous year which the companies had just
enjoyed. Granting that statistics can be manipulated by partisans, is it inconceivable that these rival claims could have
been reduced to something approaching discernible fact?

Not all the answers are easy, and some measure of strife
is the price we may have to pay for the avoidance of autoc-
racy. I do not say every strike can be avoided—or should be—
or that government in every instance can find a formula
that serves the interests of the national community without
flagrant injustice to one of the parties. I do say that obsessive,
unreasoning fear of government subjects us to needless disorder and disarray. Although I should hardly offer a precise
blueprint of a planned society that overcame anarchy in
our economic affairs, I submit that the subject should not be
deemed inappropriate for public debate. It is perhaps symptomatic of some ferment that the Democratic Advisory Coun-

cil (whose views are not to be confused with the performance
of the Democratic Party) has recently said out loud that
Jeffersonian dictum—that government is best which governs
least—may not be the supreme wisdom in the year 1959. After
all, we long ago discarded Jefferson's suggestion that a revolution every twenty years might be a salutary thing for the
body politic.

Perhaps Dr. Lewis is ahead of his time, or irrelevant to
it, but the closing words of his statement are set down here
as an incitement to public argument:

"As men ponder these matters they will not fail to be
impressed by a panoramic spectacle provided by the giant
firm itself—far-flung bureaucratic enterprises operating with
acceptable efficiency in response to a mélange of (only partially identified) motives and incentives, each enterprise held
in dubious ownership by thousands upon thousands of
persons passively quiet in their shadowy remoteness, and each
enterprise apparently quite capable, under responsible direction, of co-ordination with others in bureaucratic operation
on an even wider scale. It *could* occur to these men that
directed co-ordination, responsible under society's government to society, can be had. It could occur to them that its
achievement, far from constituting a threat to cherished
freedoms (how free is the individual who is subject to
coercion of compassionless markets or the whims of corporate conscience?), might be a wholly rewarding expression
and embodiment of freedom. As the import of these things
breaks upon them it *could* happen that a faraway expression
will steal across their faces. It *could* be that men will ask
themselves, 'Why not?' "

I know all the scare-words essayists live by, and Dr. Lewis
will no doubt find himself dismissed in most places as a

creeping socialist, or worse. But possibly it is time for some adventurous political souls to ascertain whether the old epithets are as fatal as they are presumed to be.

One need not deride the gains in national well-being that we have made to remember a lot of forgotten people. As Leon Keyserling has pointed out in an exchange with Dr. Galbraith about the use of the phrase "affluent society":

". . . in 1957 we had more than 7,000,000 consumer units (multiple-person and single-person families) with annual incomes *below* $2,000 and we had more than 19,000,000 with incomes *below* $4,000—a figure considerably below that usually established by competent agencies as the bare minimum required today for a healthy and decent standard of living. This comes to more than a quarter of multiple-person families. These families may be living in 'affluence' compared with people in India, or even compared with an even larger number of people in the U.S. a generation or two ago. *But they are certainly living in poverty by any standard that should have meaning for us today.*"

The debate between Galbraith and Keyserling largely involved priorities—whether the stimulation of the rate of economic growth should take precedence over the allocation of income and the promotion of public services. I am not concerned here with their difference; they both argue plausibly. For what is clear now is that, the way things are going, neither priority ranks high on the list of either party; both involve a degree of government intervention and federal spending that most of our political figures find personally repugnant or publicly indefensible. Not until this bogeyman is confronted, challenged and overcome in a great new national debate may we even begin to move forward on either front. We are as delinquent about the plight of migratory workers as we are about the construction of urban schools; it is still sufficient for the American Medical Association to cry socialism and spending to evoke mass salivation in Congress and thereby postpone for another year, and another and another, any major endeavor in public health.

The view of do-nothing government was most plainly stated by Secretary of Agriculture Benson when proposals for federal regulation to protect the nation's migrant workers were being advanced by Secretary of Labor Mitchell. There are half a million such workers scattered across the land, living in subhuman squalor, victims of the most wretched exploitation, obtaining average incomes of $892 a year, transported from place to place in dangerously substandard vehicles. But Mr. Benson stubbornly resisted suggestions that they be given minimal federal safeguards.

"The proposed regulations," he declared, "retain the concept of federal intervention and administrative control and regimentation that is contrary to the principles of the Administration and that is so repugnant to agriculture."

The stagnation at home mars the face that we show to the world. Mired in what has become generously known as middle-of-the-roadism, a euphemism for going nowhere at a measured pace, we quibble and quarrel about international economic efforts that mean little and less in an impoverished universe. "The percentage of our total national product which has been flowing in recent years into international economic cooperation and assistance is so imperceptible that one blushes to mention it," Keyserling wrote. But a nation that has grown indolent and indifferent in dealing with economic distress and public welfare at home is singularly ill-equipped to do much about the squalor of the underdeveloped lands. In fact it invites a resurgence of isolationism when it seems prepared for even limited undertakings abroad while practicing "economy" at home.

By contrast with much of mankind we are an island of privilege. Once again, Adlai Stevenson has noted, we have what Disraeli called "two nations" in the world at large. One, "a small minority of comparative wealth," lives mainly around the North Atlantic; its per capita income is from $600 to $2000 in a "fortunate North America." But the per capita income for two-thirds of humanity is not more than $100; in India, "the largest single democratic community in the world," the average is about $60.

"In my judgment this disparity of living standards is the most important and fateful fact in the world, today," Stevenson said.

"And the worst of it is that instead of getting better it is getting worse. The rich are getting richer and the poor poorer as population grows faster than production in the poor areas."

Shortly after Mr. Stevenson spoke those words the Democratic leaders in Congress reaffirmed their intention to slash the Administration's meager foreign-aid program and thereby establish their identity as the true "economizers."

Again our political mishmash blurs what ought to be a momentous national discussion about the scope of our commitment. The Rockefeller Reports and the Stevenson treatise reflect essentially the same spirit and approach to the role we ought to be playing in the world; but neither has had any visible impact on the thinking of the men who are writing—and rewriting—economic aid programs. It is still possible almost any day of the week to revive the ancient argument about why we lost China to Communism; but it is hard to detect any great hubbub over what ought to be done to make India's democracy a flourishing partner in

Asia. There are moments when the quest for a reduction in taxes must sound to the world as if it were the only passion in our lives, the only issue on which Americans can be stirred. Conceivably that is the case; but long years in the newspaper business also convince me that the grunts and groans of Republican editorial writers should not always be confused with the voice of America—and may not even have any direct connection with the private opinions of the fellows at the typewriter. People may properly resent tax increases when they feel they are being "had" by corrupt or indolent politicians. But they have rarely been given the case for bold new programs in any dramatic terms.

What remains to be seen is whether there is any political figure on the landscape capable of appealing to both our brains and our sentiment, audacious enough to suggest that government can again be the creature and instrument of a free people rather than their enemy, wise enough to see the inseparable link between planning at home and purposefulness in the world, adventurous enough to insist that high taxes are not an inordinate price to pay for the realization of some tranquility on earth.

It was neither an economist nor a politician but a philosopher named Irwin Edman who summed up the matter most felicitously:

"Nor need there be any fear, I think, that the planning of the instruments of living in the interests of human happiness will be an enemy of human liberty. Planning the condition by which human beings can live at all and live together does not mean prescribing what that particular kind of happiness will be. The vaunted liberties of a democratic society have been too often the liberties of the already entrenched and privileged, the economic and moral slavery of the many. To organize the means of living for all is not to preclude the possibility of living well, or variously or individually, by each. To make and secure life for all is not to destroy liberty and happiness for each; it is to promote them. Only where 'planning' becomes an end in itself, and the individual is a cog in a totalitarian machine, does organization by intelligence mean discipline by force."

CHAPTER 7

With All Deliberate Lack

of Speed

A WRY JEST is current in Southern areas where resistance to the Supreme Court's school decision is most massive.

"We will abolish our schools, if necessary, to save segregation."

"Yeah. You can. But within a few years you won't have many people who can spell the word."

—Ralph McGill, editor of the *Atlanta Constitution*.

No issue has more cruelly exposed the small political men of our time than the Negro's quest for equality. No controversy has produced larger measures of hypocrisy and guile in high places. Few episodes in our history have provoked as much adult delinquency, ranging from the ugly violence of Little Rock mobsters to the moral cowardice exhibited by the President of the United States and so many of the political eminences of both parties when confronted by the spectacle of children under fire.

To most of the ambitious men of the day, the Negro's

effort to end what Norman Cousins has called the Age of
Indignity has become an intolerable white man's burden.
It has threatened to disrupt the ancient marriage of conservative Northern Republicans and Southern Democrats.
It has cast a pall over the candidacies of many men. It has
created the kind of uneasiness that even the most cynical
adventurers experience when their pretensions are rudely
challenged.

What makes the matter so exasperating to so many men
is that it cannot be swept under the rug, even by bipartisan
agreement. It is forever intruding, upsetting the neatest
calculations of aspirants for high and low office alike, haunt-
ing the orations of precinct politicos and Secretaries of State
with fine impartiality. The guilt it stirs increases the tension
of the debate; men are never more vociferous than when
they dimly perceive their faithlessness to themselves.

Civil rights has become to the politics of the present
what the drive for union organization was to the politics of
the 1930's. The issue is both deeply moral and economic;
it involves the conscience and sense of justice of many who
do not happen to be black just as the emergence of unionism
in the mass-production industries evoked the sentimental
allegiance of many who did not happen to be industrial
workers. And, like any great issue, it brings new, irritating
complexities to the lives of simple political men, most of
whom tell themselves that everything could be quietly
worked out if "agitators" did not muddle matters by refusing to play the game and wait for the long run.

But the pace of history has quickened. It has been given
greater momentum by events beyond our borders. For one
thing, as Ralph McGill has pointed out, "across two great
wars now, we, along with other free peoples, have preached

the rights of men everywhere to be free and equal—we have encouraged long-oppressed peoples to rise." Now we are presumably engaged in a great missionary effort among the people of Asia. We are subjected to derision that is especially discomforting because it rests on so hard a core of truth.

The answers of the "gradualists" have grown steadily less satisfying. One can recite them from memory. There has been greater improvement in the status of the American Negro in the last fifteen years than in the previous fifty; we are committed as a nation to new advances; it is more important to provide adequate housing and employment opportunities for Negroes than to hasten the process of school integration; who could have imagined two decades ago that a man named Jackie Robinson would be only the first of a long line of distinguished ballplayers to win acceptance in the major leagues?

All this does come under the heading of progress. The trouble is that the premise of that progress has suddenly come into question—the premise being that the Negro is an inferior whom we shall charitably, but ever so slowly, permit a place in the sun, and who can only jeopardize his chance if he presses his claim too hard and "prematurely." We have been told that "the South" will rise up and turn back the clock unless we proceed with utmost deference to its sensitivities, and the mere statement of the proposition contains the offense, for it suggests that "the South" is something quite apart from the Negroes who live in it. In effect we have discovered that as a nation we still accept the Southern definition of the issue. During the 1940's Professor Howard Odum of North Carolina University wrote *Race and Rumors of Race* in which he asserted that the crucial problem confronting white Southerners was to "face the plain assumption that they did not appraise the Negro as the same sort of human being as they themselves are."* What has become apparent in the recent months and years of conflict is that this assumption is not restricted to the South, and that it underlies the mood and spirit with which the Negro's aspirations have been treated across the political landscape—in Northern suburbia as in the Southern city.

Now there is an incipient rebellion against that whole view of things. It is voiced most articulately by Negro spokesmen but one detects many signs of it among younger people of varied color. It is worthy of some note that 30,000 participated in a "youth pilgrimage" to Washington in 1959 imploring swifter school desegregation, and that many of the participants were white. One may observe that this is a small fragment of the younger set, but it is one of the largest signs of life exhibited by the younger generation in recent years.

More important is the phenomenon that has occurred in many schools where desegregation has taken place and where, despite the raucous preliminary noises of sections of the adult community, the transition has been placid. Such episodes offer ground for suspicion that the situation may be getting out of the elders' hands. They also invite an inquiry as to whether the advocates of timidity are behind the time. One is certainly justified in contending that the strife at Little Rock was man-made, rather than child-inspired; surely the whole course of events there would have been different if Orval Faubus had not dreamed that he was the white man's savior, and if Mr. Eisenhower's moral leadership had been as decisive as his capacity for ordering troops into action.

None of this is to say that the problems of transition are

* Quoted in *The Negro and the Schools* by Harry S. Ashmore (Chapel Hill, University of North Carolina Press, 1954).

all manufactured. The country will face long and difficult interludes before the end is sighted. The ugly resistance encountered by school authorities in New York in seeking to execute school desegregation programs through the transfer of pupils from "ghetto" areas is a measure of both the national scope of the issue and the moral illiteracy to be overcome. But we have passed the point where there can be any calm accommodation between those who still cling to the doctrine of the master race, and those who find it repugnant; there can be no enduringly jolly political truce in the interests of "party unity" between those who would stave off effective civil rights legislation and those who profess to believe in it. For there are too many places where the issue has been drawn, too much emotion is already invested in the struggle and too much of the national future is at stake. I never enjoy being told that the Negro must be accorded first-class citizenship in our society because "the world is watching us"; one likes to believe that the Christian ethic can assert itself without the Communist taunt. But the reality is that this pressure is upon us, and it eliminates any possibility of retreat.

Against that background the maneuvers and shams of most political leadership seem as puny as they are transparent. They are based on the wistful belief that this is a passing show rather than a battle of the century; the miscalculation may be the doom of many men.

Consider, for example, what happened in the Senate early in 1959 in the aftermath of the Congressional elections which allegedly produced a "liberal landslide."

The first big business before that body was a move sponsored by the enlarged and presumably rejuvenated liberal bloc to end the tyranny of the filibuster.

It was not a new effort but it was presumably being undertaken now under remarkably favorable auspices. There were bright new faces in the Democratic galaxy; they had replaced right-wing Republicans who had long aligned themselves with the Southern battalions in resisting any change in the rule.

The rule was simple. It required that two-thirds of the U.S. Senate be required to stand up to end a filibuster. With so many sturdy sons of the South occupying Senate seats, this meant that only a handful of additional votes were needed to insure the continuance of what is euphemistically called debate.

Emboldened by the November results, such earnest advocates of civil rights as Paul Douglas, Clifford Case, Hubert Humphrey and Jack Javits prepared for the showdown. Their goal was the abolition of the two-thirds provision and the establishment of majority rule.

Let it be perfectly plain that they did not call for sudden suppression of debate. The formula they advocated would actually have allowed almost two months of rhetoric before the day of reckoning. Despite much of the distorted press comment, this was not a choice between full-dress discussion and abrupt cloture. The issue was whether the Senate would ever have a chance to vote on great matters affecting the lives and liberties of the Negro populace of the South. At last the possibility of breaking the Southern stranglehold seemed to be at hand.

Enter Lyndon Johnson.

There is no contention here that Johnson is a personal villain engaged in a sinister racist conspiracy. This tall, able, amiable man from Texas is an early New Dealer whose dreamiest nostalgias concern his support for Franklin D. Roosevelt. He is a latterday statesman who deems himself deeply misunderstood by the liberal camp simply because he regards the issue of equal rights as a nuisance, a diversion, a secondary and divisive question which can best be settled by superficial gesture and postponement. If he were a Senator from New York he might have been a firebrand scorching the appeasers and compromisers who dared to tell the Negroes of America that their applications for admission to the brotherhood of man must await the approval of Brother Russell of Georgia. But he comes from Texas, and he has nothing but contempt for those who do not comprehend the complexities of a man from Texas in seeking to sponsor the admission of second-class citizens into the brotherhood.

The historic struggle was as brief as it was uninspired. In less than a week Johnson prevailed. He not only routed the majority rule provision; he similarly crushed the proposal of a Kentucky Republican—Senator Morton—for adoption of a three-fifths rule. Alternately arrogant and derisive, Johnson let it be known that he was prepared to meet the test offered by the liberals and to demonstrate their incapacity for gathering votes in a fateful hour. They had audaciously tried to play his game; let them know better next time.

His methods were as rugged as they were rhetorical. On the floor he taunted and teased; off the floor he held in his hand the vast weapon of committee assignment, of favoritism for special pieces of local legislation, the mingled inducements of promise and threat that are the possession of a majority leader. Nothing he could promise or threaten would have meant much to a man who cared deeply and passionately about the outcome. But many men did not care that deeply or passionately. New or old, they were members of the club and they had learned—whether long ago in their pre-

cinct clubs or in some other bleak hangout—that a grown
political man must never act like an idealistic boy.

So now, as on so many other earlier occasions, Johnson
carried the day and night. As so often before, it was the
technician's triumph, devoid of any lasting content. In recent
years he had never made any secret of his disdain for those
who tried to beat him at his game. The Senate was his play-
ground, and this was his show. Stricken at the age of forty-
seven by a heart attack, he had had his brush with death and
returned to the fray with less patience for those who questioned his mastery of the Senate.

What did Lyndon want? Those who tried to answer in
coldly strategic terms said he believed the real future of the
Democratic Party lay in a new alliance of South and West—
and it was such an alliance that he forged in the filibuster
conflict of January, 1959. In Johnson's view, it was said, there
could be no effective accommodation between the Southern
bloc and the Northern Senators whose constituencies included large Negro groups. But there was a substantial non-
Southern territory where no such problem existed; he would
operate there.

This puts the issue crudely, but it was the essence of the
matter. To Lyndon Johnson civil rights had become an
obsessive preoccupation of certain Eastern and Northern
groups. He did not mean to say that he was unaware of the
problem. If he had his life to live without regard to the
cruel exigencies of politics, he would no doubt have preferred to battle for equal rights for all. But that was not the
way life had been arranged for him. His strength, his survival, his position, his unique place in politics rested on
the assumption that civil rights could be deemed number
twenty-five on a list of forty-seven major national problems
and it was his intention to devote himself without fear or

fervor to a major number of those problems, not necessarily including number twenty-five.

Above all he did not intend to let the Democratic Party be torn asunder by an issue that ranked number twenty-five on his list—especially in most nonelection years.

Thus the first great civil rights debate of 1959 passed swiftly; it was all over almost as soon as it had begun. In retrospect the astonishing thing is how small a storm it created, how quickly the political sky cleared. It may be said that this proved beyond dispute that no one was deeply aroused about the strife; one might respond that people had learned not to take such encounters seriously, and that the number of men in the Senate who took it seriously in most nonelection years could meet in a very small room.

That was neither the first time (nor would it be the last) when this had occurred. There had been the great advance notices; there had been the promises of decisive conflicts to come; there had been the bitter preliminary skirmishes, the heated caucuses, the warnings of bipartisan doom. And all of this had proved to be nothing more than prelude for the arithmetical anticlimax in which Johnson won by votes of 60 to 16 and equivalents thereof.

In some journalistic places the outcome was hailed as proof that the "tyranny of the majority" had been repulsed again. After all, the sober fellows pointed out, there would be moments when lunacy would fill the national air and we would all voice prayers of thanks for the rule of reason and restraint that still endured in the Senate. (Johnson had, of course, made a minor concession; it would require only two-thirds of those present—rather than two-thirds of the full membership of the Senate—to halt debate. But this was hardly consequential, as the Southern spokesmen pointed out soon after the votes were counted; the new rule would make only the smallest fractional difference.) Democracy would still be protected against itself.

It was an argument we heard often in those hours, appealing to those whose instinctive dread of the democratic process—in matters affecting the income tax as well as the filibuster—had often been heard.

Yet, no matter how it was phrased, it was ultimately the argument that there are moments when we dare not enjoy the luxury of free government, and that we must impose a paralysis of will on ourselves to control our indiscretions.

There were more skirmishes to come, and when they were over a single legislative product had emerged; Congress voted to preserve the life of the Civil Rights Commission. But it had done nothing to alter the somber condition found in the report of that Commission released just as adjournment neared:

It is sobering to know that a substantial number of the people and of the public officials in one region do not yet accept the mandate to end racial discrimination in public education with all deliberate speed, and to know that there are a considerable number of counties where Negroes are denied the right to vote. Standing in the way of reasonable solutions to the difficulties involved in ending discrimination in all walks of our public life is the great stubborn fact that many people have not yet accepted the principles, purposes, or authority of the Fourteenth and Fifteenth Amendments . . .

Moreover, this problem is not now limited to one region. The degree of racial discrimination in the field of housing that exists throughout the country, and is particularly critical in the great metropolitan centers of the North and West, suggests unwillingness on the part of a substantial portion of Americans to follow the rule of equal rights. Concentration of colored Americans in restricted areas of most major cities produces a high degree of school segregation even in communities accepting the Supreme Court's decision. With the migration of Negroes and Puerto Ricans to the North and West, and an influx of Mexicans into the West and Southwest, the whole country is now sharing the problem and the responsibilities . . .

What is also sobering is the magnitude of the injury inflicted upon Negro Americans by the events recorded in this historical review. It is reflected in the poor education, low income, inferior housing and social demoralization of a considerable part of the Negro population. What compounds the problem is that these unfortunate results of slavery, discrimination and second-class citizenship are in turn used by some more fortunate Americans to justify the perpetuation of the conditions that caused the injury.

Something, it is said, is usually better than nothing; Johnson's pledge to return to the subject in 1960 was an acknowledgment that it could not be banished from the American agenda—especially in an election year. But it was also an attempt to provide largely rhetorical amelioration in a realm where there had been no shortage of benign verbiage. By and large the civil rights "debates" provide a chance for Northern legislators to place themselves on record in election years. Would 1960 be any different? Would Johnson's deepening Presidential aspirations (and the absence of any opponent to him in the Texas senatorial primary) persuade him that more than a token demonstration was in order? Would Northern Republicans endanger their alliances with Southern Democrats to protect the Presidential cause of Richard Nixon? All that remained to be seen. Amid the byplay and counterpoint the disheartening thing was the sense that so few men in Congress were animated by any great moral fervor, and so many were going through the motions in deference to what they contemptuously described in private as "the Negro vote," as if only a few eccentric white men could possibly feel strongly about the subject of equality.

I make no secret of my view that civil rights has become a "fighting issue" and that the discords involved in its resolution are preferable to the insufferably patronizing attitude toward a multitude of people embodied in the rituals of so-called moderation. I do not know the words which can explain to a young Negro that he is obliged to serve with equal hazard in the armed forces of the United States and accept the role of inferiority when he returns home. I do not know how he can be asked to tell his children that he has received the Distinguished Service Medal but that they are entitled only to the inferior service of segregated schools. I do not know how to tell a Negro colleague that his work is exemplary, but that I hope he will not be too aggressive about seeking an apartment in my neighborhood. I do not know how to tell American Negroes that they have been put on the waiting list for full membership in American society, but that it may take another ten or twenty years to win over some of the stuffy characters on the admissions committee.

Too often we are called upon to weigh with equal solemnity Senator Eastland's claim that he belongs to the master race against the assertion that Thurgood Marshall is as good a lawyer as any white men we have known. We are called upon to feel equal compassion for those who are tormented by the thought of their children sharing a classroom with Negroes, and for the Negro parents who do not know whether their kids will escape the mob outside the school. We are asked, in short, to balance impartially the claims of those who have designated themselves racially superior against those who are knocking on the doors of the brotherhood of man. And so, in legislative terms, we are asked to show due consideration for the lynchers as for the lynched, and to condemn as rival species of "extremist" those who uphold the law and those who defy it.

I am mindful of the dangers and ugliness of strife—and especially mindful that Negro children may most often be its victims.

But if they are capable of the valor and dignity they have exhibited, the least the rest of us can do is to avoid the appearance of being above the battle, or to display—as Mr. Eisenhower has so often done—an equal concern for the tormentors and the tormented.

Clearly the issue is charged with a special intensity. Perhaps, as the debate goes on, there will be increasing candor about its undertones. It is disingenuous for advocates of school desegregation to disclaim any vision of "social equality" for the Negro; a generation that grows up together in school will find social fraternization more and more commonplace. By the same token, the day may come when white Southerners will more frankly acknowledge the sexual hypocrisies of the structure they are trying to preserve. One need not make Freud the architect of politics to recognize the sexual tensions underlying the present conflict, and to discern the unspoken anxieties that impart so much violence to the debate.

The most complete expression of "social equality"—sexual intercourse between the races—is an old Southern custom. It is clandestine and guilt-ridden; it invites the mutual suspicion of husband and wife, because each shares the fear that the other is finding sublime gratification in the defiance of the taboo. It is not the despoiling of white Southern womanhood that is the nightmare of the segregationist, but the furtive fear that she may be enjoying it.

In a characteristically lively essay published in *The Progressive*, Milton Mayer observed:

"When the segregationist rails against 'race pollution,' he does not necessarily care how much the race is polluted or how much his ancestors have done to pollute it, as long as their legal wives were white.

"When he cries 'mongrelization,' he doesn't ordinarily mean that he objects to the production of mongrels by himself or the males who listen to him, just as long as the producers, good, religious people that they are, are married *only* in the sight of God."

A large number of American Negroes, Mayer pointed out, have one or more white ancestors; Southern segregation is "daytime segregation." Twenty-eight states, including all in the South and a few in the West, bar intermarriage by law; only four profess to outlaw interracial fornication, and make no effort to enforce the decree.

"Miscegenation," Mayer concluded, "has flourished in America as in no other country." And what the South is resisting, among other things, is what he called the "solemnization of miscegenation, and the assumption of the legal, moral and religious responsibilities that solemnization entails."

To the ancient taunt of the Southern racist—"Do you want your daughter to marry a nigger?"—the statistics suggest that one might appropriately retort: "Are you sure you know your ancestors?"

Gunnar Myrdal has remarked that "the South has an obsession with sex which helps to make this region quite irrational in dealing with Negroes generally . . . The sadistic element in most lynchings also points to a close relation between lynching and thwarted sexual urges."

There are, of course, many other aspects to the Southern

tension that have been frequently explored; the forlorn status-seeking of the impoverished whites long preceded the discovery of the status seeker by contemporary journalism. But the sexual ambivalence that gives the whole desegregation debate its quality of subdued violence is rarely examined in public discussions; when that occurs, it is usually on the vulgar, simplistic level of anti-Negro accusation.

From the viewpoint of the Negro, the depth of degradation lies in the double standard which Southern justice has so long applied to the crime of rape. Year after year Negroes in the South have been executed for the crime of raping white women—with white juries often dutifully blurring the distinction between assault and assent; never has a white man suffered a similar penalty even when found guilty of the same offense against a Negro woman.

The presumption must be that there are always extenuating circumstances when a white man finds a resisting Negro woman irresistible.

In 1959 it appeared as if the double standard might finally be broken. Four white youths were arrested and tried for the peculiarly savage rape of a Negro coed at Florida A & M University in Tallahassee. The prosecutor tried the case with earnestness and diligence; the judge blocked the usual attempts of defense counsel to befuddle the proceedings; the jury returned a verdict of guilty—but with a recommendation for mercy, which prevented the judge from handing down the death penalty. (I should interject that I have no reverence for capital punishment in general; I suggest only that, so long as it survives, it should not be reserved exclusively for Negroes.)

Many Northern newspapermen had been assigned to the trial in anticipation of a reversal of the South's ancient code. Their presence stirred a good deal of indignation among

Southern editors, many of whom intimated with varying forms of discourtesy that they ought to go back where they came from. And when, soon after the trial ended, several Negroes in Queens, New York, were accused of raping a white girl, these Southern gentlemen of the press swept into action. The Associated Press office in New York was bombarded with inquiries: How much attention were the New York papers giving this case? Were they displaying as much interest in it as they had in the unfortunate Tallahassee incident? Did they care about rape in their own backyard when committed by Negro against white?

The answers were not entirely satisfying for them because the story was, in fact, given ample notice in most New York papers. But the inquiries revealed how totally they had missed the point. Rape is gruesome and newsworthy in any setting. The question in Tallahassee, as in so many places before it, was whether rape is a more serious offense when committed by Negroes against white women than by whites against Negroes. And Tallahassee offered no new answer to that question.

Perhaps eventually it will. Not long after the verdict there two Negroes tried and convicted for rape in Florida were given life sentences, rather than the death penalty, and there was some reason to believe that the fixing of the punishment was related to the earlier sentence. To those like myself who see no cures in the institution of capital punishment, the ending of the double standard by the tacit abandonment of the death penalty in all such cases could be a happy ending. But it remains to be seen whether this is what has happened, and whether the Florida pattern will be duplicated in other Southern states.

If such progress occurs, some debt is owed to the "interventionists" who focused attention on the disparity in Flor-

ida justice. It is an old Southern cliché that all things would evolve harmoniously and well if the damyankees would avoid interference in the sovereign affairs of Southern states.*
In practice, however, the impulse to "show" the North that it has misjudged its Southern brethren often seems a more compelling force than local instinct.

This is no sermon to the South. The battle for equality is national; the Northern compromisers—Democratic and Republican alike—are often morally more vulnerable than those Southerners who, at considerable private risk, have challenged, even in whispered tones, the racist rules of their environment. What I reject is the view that the North must remain silent about Southern injustice until its own hands are meticulously cleansed. There were also those who told us that we dare not speak out against Hitlerism until every vestige of prejudice had been banished from our soil, or that we have no right to challenge the Russian terror in Hungary as long as we permit any suppression of dissent at home. These are the non sequiturs that rationalize passivity.

Freedom is scarcer in Moscow than in Mississippi, and in Mississippi than in Manhattan; there is no reason for contentment about any of them. If the Russians profess to treat all men as equals, but some a little more equal than others, it is the equality of a common bondage; but that makes the mass indignities of Mississippi no prettier, nor the unofficial and unauthorized inequities of New York more tolerable.

We do not need more excuses for acquiescence. Nor do we need more "moderates" to tell us that all will be well if we proceed with all deliberate lack of speed. I confess to a deep skepticism about Northern statesmen who discover in times of political stress that their own hands are soiled, and

* In the generations before abolitionism, no Southern state made any move to abolish the institution of slavery or to mitigate its evils.

that the North must cure all its derelictions before we do battle with Southern racism. Of course it would be well if we all were morally lily-white. But the indisputable fact is that our Northern institutions of law are dedicated to the goal of equal justice, while most of the machinery of Southern government is organized to perpetuate white supremacy.

When a Northern politician abruptly discovers sin on our side of the Mason-Dixon line, I fear that he is winking at the Southern delegations, and expressing assurance that he will in no way pose a serious challenge to Southern things as they are.

On the whole I agree with Harry Golden that what has been most remarkable in this period of tension is that the Negroes have refused to do wrong. They and their children have been the victims of sadistic violence, legal subterfuge, government betrayal; in the face of each rejection and rebuff they have simply said they will seek new recourse within the framework of our Constitution, and they have patiently initiated the new steps designed to achieve what they deem to be justice. One tragedy of the white South is that it has so far produced no outstanding enlightened leader graced with the wisdom and restraint of Reverend King and equally capable of rallying opinion.

It is no disparagement of legal argument, I trust, to say that the condition with which we are dealing is morally intolerable and that a remedy must be sought which does not indefinitely postpone a day of reckoning. The "gradualists" have had their day, and it is ending. For the moment the fakers may seem to dominate the field; Senator Dirksen had the audacity in September, 1959, to assert that the Republican Party has never "played politics" with civil rights. One could cite comparable pomposities from the Democratic side of the aisle. But all of the rhetoric and maneuver seemed strangely secondary, in the winter of 1960, to the stoic valor of the young Negroes who stood passively at segregated Southern lunch counters enduring vile taunts and physical attack, and turning the other cheek. Suddenly it no longer seemed terribly important that Lyndon Johnson was now paying election-year obeisance to civil rights legislation while his Southern brethren launched their last-gasp filibuster. The thrust was already deeper, and the issue of technical legal protection was dwarfed again by the cry for a full measure of equality.

In the final analysis it may be fundamentally a matter of whether political men give a damn, whether they are able to look a Negro in the eye and tell him they will get him a membership card in the human fraternity if he just doesn't make any vulgar sounds outside the clubhouse, and that his children may one day live down their choice of parentage.

CHAPTER 8

Press-Time as Usual

WHAT I have been trying to say along most of the way is that much of the zest and intensity has gone out of our political life in an age when, as Arthur Schlesinger, Jr., once remarked, the bland have been leading the bland. Nowhere is the condition more apparent than in a large part of the daily press and in the mass-media magazines.

Once upon a time journalism was viewed as something more than an instrument for the recording of the detailed play-by-play of history and the affirmation of respectable positions. Editors fought for seemingly unpopular, even hazardous causes and reveled in the combat; they even fought with each other. All that now seems very long ago.

Most of the deans of the profession are now alternately engaged in mutual admiration exercises, the quadrennial crusade for the election of a Republican president and the discovery of safe postures which spare them any conflict with large advertisers or commanders of the American Legion. Sadly enough, few of them are suffering any real pain, because they find themselves in substantial agreement with the conservative pressure-boys. The victims of the arrangement are the members of their staffs, so many of whom have not yet made the adjustment to the orthodox Republican politics of their elders.

Given the present blurred distinctions between the parties, there is nothing inherently virtuous about a newspaper that pledges itself to the Democrats, right or wrong. Some of our most benighted racist Southern dailies have remained faithfully in the Democratic columns.

But where much of the press most pointedly reveals its spiritual decline is in the nonconfrontation of issues, and this is only partially a result of excessive commitment to the incumbent Republican Administration. There was no partisan issue involved in the Eastland committee's assault on the *New York Times;* the leader of the assault was nominally a Democrat. Yet in the face of that attack there was a monumental display of editorial apathy.

It happened in the winter of 1956. The Eastland committee (formally the Senate Internal Security Subcommittee) had been running out of headlines for a long time; there was also reason to believe that its chairman felt aggrieved over the vigorous civil rights editorials which the *Times* had been publishing. Whatever the motivation, it became known one day that the subcommittee had undertaken an investigation of "Communism in the press" and had selected the *Times* as its target.

In another time the mere announcement of the move would have stirred a national upheaval. For decades the press of the land had thundered with a single voice when any man sought to abridge the liberty of one of its members. Indeed, the sound of the war cry—"freedom of the press"—was sufficient to rejuvenate even the stodgiest elders of the profession and bring them to the scene of battle.

Now came the Eastland subcommittee, hunting down a handful of members of the vast *Times* staff, some of whom

were admittedly ex-Communists, even extending its researches to the composing room (who knows how a typo-
graphical error might undermine the national security?), and
questioning them not merely about their alleged private
political affiliations but, in at least one case, closely examin-
ing the dispatches a man had filed for veiled evidence of
subversion.

It is surely unnecessary to argue here the substantive question of the *Times*'s virtue; if there are those who suspect that
the good, gray lady has a scarlet streak, they are beyond the
reach of my voice. Moreover, it is my view of the First
Amendment to the Constitution that the *Times* would have
full liberty to become a mouthpiece for Fascists, Communists
or vegetarians if its directors were disposed to do so; and
that unless they violated the law—through, say, the deliberate
disclosure of top military secrets—there was nothing Congress
could properly do about it.

All this once seemed to be elementary, but it wasn't in
1956 and perhaps it is not today. In 1956 (as, if I may say
so, in 1953, when the *Post* came under somewhat comparable
attack from the McCarthy committee) the old battle cry had
lost its fire, and many of the venerable warriors were missing
in action. Not long after Mr. Eastland and his men had
begun their degrading assault on the *Times* staff men, the
Post conducted a poll of 190 newspapers published daily in
the nation's 100 largest cities. Our question was: What editorial position had they taken on the Eastland foray?

The answers revealed that 112 out of the 190 had maintained total editorial silence about this unpleasantness; 35
were critical of the subcommittee in varying degrees; 33
found justification for the inquiry; 10 managed to discuss
the subject without indicating any clearly defined attitude.

Most of those who defended the inquiry argued that, if it

was all right for Congressional committees to haul in professors, bricklayers and village idiots for scrutiny of their political views—and they felt it was all right—then there was no reason for the press to claim any exemption. There is a certain legal logic to this view. Perhaps a commendable candor would have added that, since most newspapers had long ago abandoned any real resistance to the business of political inquisition, the press had no ground for insisting that it be left alone. The great concessions had been made long before when we accepted as a nation the proposition that the threat of Communism required the sacrifice of the principle of political privacy, and that any old-fashioned character who clung to the principle of the secret ballot was under suspicion.

What is most striking about the poll, however, is not the number of papers which defended the inquiry or the number which condemned it, but the silence which 112 of these metropolitan newspapers—58 percent of the total examined—were able to sustain throughout this episode. I can only guess that some of the silent ones chose not to speak simply because discretion had become the commonplace editorial habit in all areas allegedly touching that dread domain called security.

The *Times* survived. While a few of its staff suffered prolonged harassment as a result of their invocation of the First Amendment, there were those who serenely pointed out soon afterward that the whole incident was relatively trivial because all the news that was fit to print was still being printed. But that was not the point. For one thing there would be no way of measuring how many other editors and publishers might be subtly affected by this intimidatory excursion. What mattered even more was the revelation of the degree to which the sickness of "non-speak" had afflicted the lords and ladies of the press in questions deeply involving the liberties of Americans.

A more recent example of the ailment occurred in 1958 when the *Post* began preparation of a series of articles on FBI Director J. Edgar Hoover. Of all the sacred cows of American journalism, Mr. Hoover is almost certainly the holiest. The immunity he has achieved from criticism of any sort can hardly be ascribed to the diligence with which he performs his labors. Other bureaucrats have worked long days and nights without enjoying such freedom from close scrutiny. The caution of some legislators in discussing his works may be due to the apparently well-founded fear that the FBI has taken pains to explore their histories, and what Congressman has no secret in his life that could not be used against him some time of some day? Perhaps some journalists are inhibited by the same dark thought, but the general reticence, I think, is primarily a tribute to the far-flung public relations operation which has grown up around the FBI. It includes columnists and correspondents whom the FBI intermittently favors with small special disclosures, it includes eminent religious personages, it includes Senators and Congressmen, some of whom may retain some private skepticism about Mr. Hoover's perfection but learned long ago that his birthday is no less proper an occasion for special tribute on the floor of Congress than George Washington's.

Out of this circle of worship has emerged the proposition that criticism of any phase of the works of Mr. Hoover or the FBI is prima facie evidence of subversion, and that he who indulges in such irreverence is a man to be watched. It is true that Mr. Hoover is fond of saying that he welcomes "constructive criticism" but there is no evidence that he has ever found any criticism constructive; he is equally fond of warning in the same paragraph that agents of the Kremlin are busily fomenting campaigns of hate against him and the men who toil for him.

All that being known, we anticipated that publication of an irreverent series would produce the kind of attack that has been directed against the few who had previously attempted an unromanticized portrait. We did not quite anticipate that the attack would begin within a matter of days after the first reporter had conducted the first interview with the first prospective source.

At once Senator John Martin Butler, Maryland Republican and member of the Senate Internal Security Subcommittee, charged that "a deliberate smear campaign" was under way against Mr. Hoover. He indicated that a Senate investigation might well be in order "because the American people are entitled to know the origin of the campaign, who is behind it and how it is financed" and he added:

"I am reliably informed that reporters for the *Post* are seeking out former FBI agents and asking the most repulsive questions imaginable concerning Mr. Hoover. No self-respecting newspaper would permit such suggestive questions to be asked."

In his zeal Mr. Butler did Mr. Hoover a disservice; no sinister lines of personal inquiry were being pursued, and Mr. Butler must be aware that the laws are abundant protection against private slander for even a lesser personage than the Director of the FBI. The significant thing is that a Senate investigation of a newspaper series was being proposed—before a word of that series had been written.

Mr. Butler's words were echoed soon after by Preston J. Moore, National Commander of the American Legion who was quoted this way by the Associated Press:

"Former FBI agents have been approached recently by reporters of the New York *Post*, seeking derogatory material on J. Edgar Hoover . . . Apparently forgetting, at least momentarily, that they were supposed to obtain information, not reveal it, reporters for the paper disclosed to unquestionably reliable New York sources that the *Post* planned to assign reporters to Washington, D.C., and other cities to skulk around restaurants and other places in hope of digging up information that could be used against Hoover and the FBI."

There followed a series of articles by Archbishop Cushing of Boston, widely displayed by the Hearst newspapers, "exposing" an incipient journalistic plot against Mr. Hoover; the *Journal-American,* Hearst's New York afternoon newspaper, promptly assigned Bob Considine to write an ostensibly affectionate (if at times inadvertently humorous) series eulogizing the FBI Director in particular and G-men in general; the news letter of the National Association of Manufacturers solemnly warned its subscribers to beware of an approaching critique of Mr. Hoover from palpably un-American sources; Representative Scherer similarly alerted his colleagues in the House and sent franked copies to his constituents.

Thus, through these many manifestations of the Society for the Enshrinement of J. Edgar Hoover, notice was served that the projected study should be discounted in advance, its authors damned in advance, small children guarded from exposure to the contents and grown Congressmen mobilized for battle. Throughout the storm an editorial in the *Washington Post and Times-Herald* raised a lonely dissent against the hysterics, asserting that Mr. Hoover's province was as legitimate a domain of newspaper inquiry as any other governmental sphere. Perhaps there were a few other scattered echoes of the same view which eluded me. But the general silence was deafening.

In a recent symposium published by *American Editor,* organ of the New England Society of Newspaper Editors, Ladd Hamilton of the Lewiston (Idaho) *Morning Tribune* suggested that one definition of a liberal newspaper is that "it believes the police must constantly be kept at bay. It respects Mr. J. Edgar Hoover but is not awed by him. . . ." One wonders how many newspapers live by even that modest declaration of independence.

Just how sacrosanct the FBI had become was even more fully dramatized when the *Post's* series on the FBI Director and his agency was published. The series was preceded by a two-article recital by Publisher Dorothy Schiff describing the attempts of Mr. Hoover to use advertising pressure to prevent publication of the articles. In a sense this disclosure was more important than the series itself; one of our central, if undramatic, findings was that as a personality Mr. Hoover is a comparatively uninteresting man, which makes all the more remarkable the legend associated with his name but hardly provides very exciting copy.

Yet the publisher's description of the Hoover-inspired campaign to suppress the series was greeted with almost total silence in most of the press. Let a Congressman from Podunk try to intimidate a publisher from Squedunk and the boards of the American Society of Newspaper Editors and the American Newspaper Publishers Association will rise up in emergency protest. Let a newspaper be suppressed in Batavia, and the alarums are loud. But let Mr. Hoover engage in the crudest sort of pressure, as he did in this instance, and suddenly the nation's editorial pages find themselves absorbed with censorship of the press in Turkey.

It is not my thesis that Hoover is hero or villain, but that he has escaped the examination to which government officials in a democracy ought to be subjected; the oversight is especially lamentable when it is the head of a national secret police agency who is the beneficiary of such indulgence.

Shortly before the TV scandals of 1959, Mr. Hoover, in an interview with a reporter for the *Morning Telegraph,* the racing newspaper, took part in this colloquy:

Q. Mr. Hoover, have you engaged in sports yourself and are you interested in other sports besides racing?

A. Yes, I tried tennis, but to play well took too much time . . . I like baseball and football as spectator sports, and I even like to look at the wrestling matches on TV. Maybe wrestling is or isn't on the up-and-up. I wouldn't know and I care less because on TV it's a good show and that's what I look at it for—a good show.

The interview was published in September, 1959, and the exchange was recorded in the *Post* series. But in that autumn of national uproar over TV "fixes," Mr. Hoover's indiscretion was generally ignored by a press that was addressing itself day after day to the moral problems of "rigging." The example is cited only because it is the most recent instance in which Mr. Hoover has led a charmed life in his relationship with the press.

Newspapers vary in style, technique and tone from city to city and town to town. Obviously the generalizations so far made do not apply to all, and do an injustice to the isolated figures who still cherish their independence. I know that such men exist; they simply happen to be less and less representative of a press which is overwhelmingly owned and operated by conservative Republicans (or conservative Southern Democrats) who fix the basic rules and determine the limits of political debate. And I use the word "fix" advisedly.

Plainly it is a freer press than any existing in Communist

or Fascist countries, where editors share the common slavery of the populace, but that is no ground for continuous self-congratulation.

It is a press that has grown generally comfortable, fat and self-righteous and which, with noteworthy exceptions, voices the prejudices and preconceptions of entrenched wealth and caste rather than the passion for justice which we associate with our best journalistic traditions.

It is a press generally more concerned with the tax privileges of fat cats than with the care and feeding of any underdog.

It is a press that confuses independence with the economic rights of ownership and too often feels a furtive kinship with the manifesto voiced by Thomas Waring, editor of the *News and Courier* in Charlestown, S.C.:

"Though our country may be spared firing squads and barb-wire camps, tax bills are already biting deep into the personal property of the citizens. Property rights are an essential part of civil rights. Men will die to protect their property.

"If the American Republic already has passed into the democratic phase—meaning that the mob has begun to rule —the dictator cannot be far behind."

It is a press far more forthright in combating tyranny in Hungary than in waging the fight for freedom in the United States.

I have already indicated what I mean by saying that the predominantly conservative press fixes the rules of debate. It does so by obeisance to such untouchables as Hoover, J. Edgar (and Hoover, Herbert), or by use of the word "planning" as an epithet. It also does so by the selection of its spheres of interest, and by the exclusion of some issues from the public forum. Under Eisenhower, our Far Eastern policy, as noted in an earlier chapter, has been largely exempted from the free-for-all of press controversy. During the 1956 campaign it became almost an impropriety to prolong discussion of the President's health, as if it were apparent that a heart attack and ileitis were exactly the prescription for occupancy in the White House.

I rejoiced when Dave Beck and his boys were exposed by a Senate committee, and I trust the day has passed when liberals endow corrupt labor leaders with the status of sacred cow. But it was in the same interval that an abortive Senate inquiry into the machinations of the oil lobby occurred. It perished with hardly a word of mourning from the same press which has derived so much headline fun out of disclosure of union corruption. The special tax privileges still accorded the oil industry under the benign rule of the Texas Congressional leadership (and the Texan in the White House) contain the makings of a national scandal; but the scandal remains hidden because only a handful of newspapers from coast to coast even pretend to care.

The Legion of Decency marches on, imposing its own standards of virtue on the rest of the community. When it sought, with the help of Cardinal Spellman, to impose a ban on the film *Baby Doll* in enlightened old New York, the editorial pages were distinguished by almost total speechlessness. Even the spacious editorial columns of the *Times* found no room for the controversy. Ironically, the issue was debated with conspicuous freedom in many Catholic publications even while most nonsectarian editors and publishers were paralyzed by fear of offense to the "Catholic vote." In Syracuse both daily newspapers—the *Post-Standard* and the *Herald Journal*—rejected all ads for the movie, a capitulation which was perhaps more honorable than the performance of other papers in other places which first accepted the ads and then declined to resist the censors.

Birth control also ranks high on the list of taboo matters. When the Roman Catholic Bishops of the U.S. thrust the subject into the front pages by denouncing what they called a "systematic propaganda campaign" for planned parenthood, there was a momentary flurry; the excitement, of course, was increased because the declaration focused the cameras on Senator Kennedy at a moment when his Presidential ambitions were very much involved. Kennedy responded by saying that he was opposed to U.S. advocacy of birth control and the use of federal funds for such programs; other candidates cautiously observed that they did not believe we should "impose" such plans on other peoples but that we should not withhold funds for these purposes if they were requested. Virtually no one chose to debate the Bishops' statement that it would be equally improper to provide "public assistance" to promote "artificial birth prevention" within the U.S. Did this mean an opposition to federal grants for hospitals in which birth control information was made available to those whose lives might be imperiled by pregnancy? Presumably it did; but political leaders preferred not to explore such ramifications of the question and most of the press seemed equally reticent about pursuing them. Many newspapers met the whole problem editorially by acting as if it had not arisen, or by observing that there was much to be said on all sides, and perhaps the less said the better.

There was earlier reference to the timidity with which much of the press has approached the fateful matters of nuclear tests and fallout. In part this may have simply reflected a reluctance to deal with the complexities of a subject that might be called over our heads; the President had made it plain in 1956 that he resented popular debate over the continuance of the tests; and when, at one point, the *Times* reported that the Administration had been seriously contemplating a test moratorium prior to Mr. Stevenson's advocacy of the move, few newspapers displayed any curiosity about this extraordinary hint of atomic politics.

As Earl Ubell, science editor of the *Herald Tribune,* noted in a broadcast in 1959:

"The National Association of Science Writers and, indeed, the Atomic Energy Commission itself have made two surveys which show definitely that at least one-third of the nation does not know and has never heard—I have to repeat that— has never heard—of radioactive fallout from an atomic bomb. Furthermore, only about 12 percent of the population really knows, technically, what it is about—and when I say technically, I mean it on the lowest level of understanding. The reasons for this are many and varied but we can see that the public does not have much, if any, information in this field to make intelligent decisions."*

One may acknowledge a certain instinctive public tendency to avoid close entanglement with fallout data, just as heavy smokers may often decline to read all the detailed medical testimony indicating a linkage between lung cancer and cigarettes. But Ubell's statistics also say something about the extent to which the press has generally given only routine and unimaginative coverage to the fallout story, and in practice, if not by deliberate design, accepted the Administration's long-held view that this territory is off limits.

In the 1940's, when I was a Washington correspondent, I

---

* From the transcript of a series of TV programs on The Press and the Public produced by WGBH-TV Mass., with Louis Lyons as moderator and with the sponsorship of the Fund for the Republic.

first heard Sir Willmott Lewis, then the distinguished Washington correspondent of the London *Times,* observe that it was the function of a newspaper "to afflict the comfortable and comfort the afflicted" and I have never heard any nobler description of our calling. But in fact most of the press has been afflicted with comfortableness and the "troublemaker" is an unwelcome character around most city rooms. Many newspapers are now owned and run by men and women whose sole or primary concern is the business office, whose driving mission is to avoid any escapades that might disturb the serene flow of profits, and whose personal conservatism in politics coincides happily with the predilections of the major advertisers.

So most of what still poses as newspaper "crusading" journalism is safely restricted to those crusades which harmonize with the interests of the conservative business community, or are simply irrelevant to it. In the summer of 1959, for example, the New York *World-Telegram and Sun* (Scripps-Howard) and the *Journal-American* (Hearst) embarked on parallel—nay, competitive—"crusades" to save the nation from inflation. Each exhorted their readers to deluge their Senators and Congressmen with coupons (provided for their convenience) calling upon them to stand firm against the monster. But neither newspaper ever acknowledged that effective resistance to inflation might conceivably mean government control of prices or governmental intervention in the affairs of industry and management. Both directed all their fury against "government spending"—the current point at issue being the scope of the federal housing bill under debate in Congress, with the President striving to render even more boneless the skeletal legislation presented to him.

Neither newspaper took any serious cognizance of the suggestion by Congressman—and former OPA Director—Chester

Bowles that the greatest anti-inflation measure of the moment might be an agreement by the steel industry to reduce prices in return for a temporary wage freeze. These newspaper crusades were entirely specialized; they were primarily aimed at government welfare programs; they could be joyously acclaimed by the same business groups which had long fought any governmental interference with inflationary price policies.

The conflict over labor legislation in the summer of 1959 demonstrated anew the surviving editorial lust of many newspapers for an old-fashioned drive against unions. Although the point must have been lost on many newspaper readers, the issue was not whether corrupt and oppressive union practices should be subjected to legislative control; the issue was whether legislation ostensibly framed to achieve those results should in fact obstruct the efforts of unions to organize workers still unorganized. That was the heart of the difference between the Landrum-Griffin bill and the more moderate measures before the House. But most of the press had little appetite for "moderation" on this front. There was a concerted rallying behind the extreme Landrum-Griffin measure, product of the perennial meeting of minds between conservative Republicans and Southern Democrats. There was great journalistic acclaim when the President, who had so often avowed his reluctance to comment on "pending" legislation, took the air to tell the country that not since Gettysburg had we confronted so grave a decision, a desecration of history of which even the National Association of Manufacturers had been incapable.

Most memorable about the episide insofar as the press was concerned was a sequel to it. When the measure passed the House James B. Carey, president of the International Union of Electrical Workers, wrote a heated letter to those members of the House who had voted for the bill, warning them that organized labor would try to remember their names and insure their defeat when they came up for re-election. Nothing in Carey's letter departed from the dictum of a noted conservative leader of U.S. labor, the late Samuel Gompers: "punish your friends and reward your enemies." But from most editorial pages and the halls of Congress came sonorous denunciation of Carey for allegedly seeking to "intimidate" the upright men who had cast their votes against "the labor lobby."

Rarely has so spurious a naïveté been imposed on the country. The truth was that the labor bills had been the signal for a great pushing-and-shoving match between the labor lobby and the business pressure groups, with both sides threatening reprisals, as they have been doing for a long time. But only one side of the story was told in most of the U.S. press.

Few papers, for example, told the story of the pressures put on Representative Erwin Mitchell of Dalton, Ga., the youngest of that state's ten-member delegation to Congress and the only one to stand out against the Landrum-Griffin Bill. There was the letter he received from E. T. Bawick, owner of the largest textile mills in his district:

"I personally spent time, money and energy getting you elected. . . . I can assure you that I will devote 100-fold more energy, time and money in getting you out if you support the kind of legislation [the more balanced Elliott bill] you announce in your letter."

Day and night during the critical days before the vote, Mitchell recounted, he was summoned to the phone by representatives of his local chamber of commerce, by other manufacturers and representatives of manufacturers warning him that his political life would be worth little if he defied the business lobby. Plainly this was not an isolated case, but to most of the big and little dailies and the great press associations, it was Carey's letter of "intimidation" that came under the heading of large news.

I have no doubt that sentiment for some legislation to curb autocratic union rule was widespread and warranted. The press diverted this sentiment into an unholy war, blurring the crucial distinctions between the various bills offered and creating the impression that "the labor bosses" were unanimously fighting legitimate restrictions no less than oppressive gimmicks. Noteworthy, too, was the fashion in which so many publishers and editors who damn "government control" in such areas as prices clamored for the severest dose of the stuff when it involved the regulation of unions. Abruptly all the old clichés were turned off. Now it was government's duty, it was government's responsibility, it was government's mission to impose its restraining hand. And the President who had intoned that peacetime government regulation of the price of steel would end the American system led the pack.

In the great majority of newspapers what remains of the crusading tradition is, in short, largely governed by a double standard. Let the press be zealous in its exposure of liberal Democrats and of labor; but let it treat carefully, if at all, in dealing with conservative Republican administrations or with the pillars of business.

In a thoughtful essay published in The Nieman Reports in January, 1959 (and later included in a volume called *The Waist-High Culture*), Thomas Griffith wrote:

"No role satisfies the newspaperman more than that of redressor; the chance to be angry, to rout out the rotten; but newspapers, being what they are, angers are grooved—confined principally to what can be found out, or if not found out, suspected to be wrong with government. Many, though not all, reporters willingly accepted this role against the Democrats, only to be disillusioned when publishers proved not such ardent pursuers of error in a Republican administration. . . .

"Unjustified waste in business, as much as a government's taxation, grabs at the public's pocketbook—but it is not generally considered fair game for newspapermen.

"Business is a privileged sanctuary, even when its institutional ads are picturing it as just a collection of open-faced 'folks' like you and me, interested in nothing but the American way, the improvement of product and the remembrance of millions of fond little shareholders . . . It remains for an occasional outburst of grudge by a disappointed contender, a stockholder's fight or—long after the event—a Congressional committee investigation, for anything adverse to be heard . . .

"A journalist too energetic in seeking out the malpractice of business risks condemnation as being against business itself, yet the same logic should apply that applies to government, that it operates best in the public interest when made to operate in the spotlight."

Perhaps the highest tribute one can pay to *Time* Magazine, where Griffith has worked as a senior editor for many years, is that he felt free to publish these words without any fear of reprisal but, also, alas, without any sign that his superiors had been moved by them. For *Time* is as clear an example of double-standard journalism as any in the land, and no textbook of modern journalism could avoid a long look at the way *Time* plays the game.

Time has been harassed by the surveillance of liberal journalists for a long time, and a number of these studies could provide the outline for the textbook chapter. One was done by Alvin Davis of the *Post,* another by Ben H. Bagdikian of the *Providence Journal.* Both owed a heavy debt to a research project conducted by Milton S. Gwirtzman, a member of the staff of the Harvard *Crimson* back in 1955. Gwirtzman concerned himself with what Bagdikian called the changeability of truth in *Time's* pages or, in the old phrase, it depends whose ox is gored.

Thus this was the way *Time* viewed the income tax on March 10, 1952, in the time of Harry Truman:

"This week, once again, the American taxpayer . . . was working over his income tax return. He did not do the job happily. . . . The blow, in full and crushing measure, now lands each March 15 on the chin of a fellow named John Q."

But this is how *Time* heralded the moment of fiscal truth in the age of Eisenhower, April 18, 1955:

". . . 60 million Americans have by this week signed their 1954 income tax forms . . . They did this, wonderful to tell, without riots or protest . . . It has become more and more unfashionable to criticize the income tax level."

Consider the transformation wrought in George E. Allen. *Time,* August 12, 1946:

"Last week . . . the President [Truman] eased his croniest crony, George E. Allen, into the Board of Directors of Reconstruction Finance Corporation." On Jan. 28, 1946: "George is all the more remarkable because, to the naked eye, he is a clown."

Eight years later George E. Allen was still around the White House. On December 14, 1954, *Time* reported without a trace of disrespect:

"Last week . . . the President [Eisenhower] chatted quietly with . . . golfing companion George E. Allen, Washington lawyer and friend of Presidents."

During the 1956 campaign *Time* impatiently brushed

aside questions about the President's health, announcing that Ike himself had resolved such inquiries "with the simplicity and finality of a one-foot putt." But by March, 1958, *Time* was cautiously conceding that "the cumulative effect of his three major illnesses had sapped his second-term strengths . . ."

Time is often lively and sometimes provocative; its vulnerability is its pretense. *Time* does not come to us saying, look, for better or for worse, we are skilled technicians serving as house organ of the Republican Party; admire our virtuosity if not our virtue; recognize that not all of us in the world are free to do what we want and support our children in the style to which we want them to become accustomed. It comes to us rather in tones of omniscience and certitude, finding character defects in those whom its partisanship would exile, and rugged simplicity of soul in those whom Mr. Luce's Republican politics makes the man of a given hour, such as Eisenhower.

It is from that stance that *Time* renders judgments about the national mood at any moment, pretending with slick self-confidence that its editors and reporters have savored and studied the American attitude when in fact they have been trying to read Mr. Luce's mind at a particular moment in history. One often wonders whether this is what Mr. Luce wants, or whether he is sometimes an innocent victim of the deception. In a way all of this is a pity; obviously it did not have to happen this way, and the magazine's resources for ascertaining more complex and varied truths than those it provides are vast. It is hard to think of any establishment in which so much talent engages in so much labor to produce so politically stacked a product, and where so much cynical mischief is done with so much dexterity.

Certainly no publication more completely epitomizes the

double standard and the fixing of the boundaries of debate
to which I have referred. Let Congressman Jinks of Minnesota decide that the issue of nuclear tests is the great one of
our time and somehow manage to explode the issue on the
floor of Congress at a time when the Republican Administration has barred the subject from discussion; the *Time* men
will take care of him something like this:

Fresh-faced freshman Jo Jinks, nasal-toned, metaphor-
spouting, dropped his bombshell on the floor of Congress
last week. It was, agreed Washington observers, the fuddiest
dud of the decade.

End of Mr. Jinks, end of argument.
But let another young man take the Washington floor in
tune with *Time*; it will come out something like this:

In the glum humdrum of heat-struck Washington, a sharp,
cool voice could be heard last week. It was that of keen-eyed
freshman Congressman Hi Jinks of Minnesota, a newcomer
who has not yet learned to be coy. In language such as the
Sputnik-shaken Capitol hadn't heard in many a moon, he said
bluntly: "It is time we looked to our defenses." And Washington observers agreed that, whatever might happen in the
race for outer space, Hi Jinks was on his way up.

Whenever serious students of the press gather, there are
melancholy recitatives about the menace of "sensationalism"
in journalism. What I have to say in these ensuing para-
graphs must be frankly labeled self-serving, because the newspaper which I edit is not only tabloid in size but also engages
in extensive coverage of what some choose to call "sensa-
tional" news and what we describe as "human-interest
stories."

I preface these remarks by saying the obvious: if there were no *New York Times,* it would have to be invented, and until it was, life would be almost unbearably difficult for those of us who run afternoon papers in New York. I concede ungrudgingly that no paper in the world makes a more conscientious effort to cover so much of the serious business of the universe, and I trust it will not be too long before that distinguished fellow known as "the gentleman from the *Times*" is filing dutifully, and at length, from other planets, and with that degree of reliability which makes his words safe for rewriting by the early-morning toilers on afternoon papers.

But to recognize the unique eminence of the *Times* is not to concede that journalism would have fulfilled all its potential role in American life if the *Times,* or some replica thereof, and nothing else, were published in every city. That would be a good thing, but it would not be the whole story of humanity in the middle of the twentieth century.

The news columns of the *Christian Science Monitor* totally reject the existence of murder, rape, incest, adultery and other such doleful tidings; they are dedicated, in effect, to the chronicle of the strivings of man as a political and cultural animal. The *Times* concedes, usually in obscure places, that the animal is more complicated, and, when he gets really out of hand, it may even give him an occasional front-page notice. But essentially the premise of such newspapers, whether carried to the *Monitor's* extreme or in the *Times's* more modest application of the same view, is that there is something improper about the use of newsprint for the unveiling of what might be called the private, as distinguished from the public, activity of the species.

Throughout the profession this view of life is accorded mingled awe and reverence, and journalism students are told

in effect that success in life means the achievement of that
degree of fiscal stability which permits a newspaper to employ the same standards of exclusion that govern the news
columns of the *Times,* if not those of the *Monitor.*

But with the already-stated respect I hold for the positive services rendered by both papers, I seriously question
whether such puritanism per se—I know of no more precise
phrase to characterize this policy—is unalloyed virtue. In a
decade, for example, which sociology may remember most
clearly for the emergence of the Kinsey reports on the sexual
behavior of American males and females, the files of the
Times seem full of omissions and inadequacies. Surely they
would be painfully meager material for any historian trying
to describe what life was really like in America at this juncture.

Whether some people like it or not, there has been a
drastic transformation amounting to a minor cultural revolution in American attitudes toward public discussion of
sexual affairs. A survey by *Newsweek* indicated how signifi-
cantly this change had altered the character of magazines
which prided themselves on their acceptability inside the
home. Within a brief interlude, *Reader's Digest* was favor-
ing its readers with an essay entitled "Achieving Sexual Harmony in Marriage," *McCall's* was explaining why "Honey-
moons Can Be a Menace to Marriage," the *Ladies' Home
Journal* was discussing "Sex and Religion: the Challenge of
Chastity" and *Cosmopolitan* was telling "Why Husbands
Disappear." In the category of less venerable but still respectable publications, *Pageant* was issuing a recipe on "How to
Overcome 'Sex Fatigue'" while *Coronet* was exploring
"Wives and the 'Middle-Age Crush.'" Even so pridefully
wholesome a journal as the *American Girl,* published by
the Girl Scouts of America, could be found discussing the

plaintive plea of a twelve-year-old girl: "Is there anything at all I can do to make my bosom grow?" (No clear-cut formula was offered.)

So-called tabloid journalism can be maudlin, surface, one-dimensional; when it is, it can be simply a daily variation of *True Confessions* or of *Hollywood Romance*. Its deficiencies can be painful and flagrant. But that is not because it deals with intimacies and aberrations, but because it too often deals with them according to lazy city-desk formulae rather than with the curiosity any writer ought to bring to his craft. In part the pressure of speed makes it easier to write the sentimental surface story rather than to find some glimpse of truth, and nothing can be more unsatisfying than the "human-interest" feature so barely human that it is unworthy of interest.

Granting all these failures, I am astonished when serious prophets of the profession deplore what they term the efforts of newspapers to "entertain" rather than to "enlighten." It is as if the enlightened man were he who had been spared all news of crime on his block, who assumed that homosexuality was an obscure ailment confined to an infinitesimal portion of alien characters, who could not believe that the nice girl down the street was convalescing from an abortion after an unfortunate affair with a man twice her age, and finally exploded with disbelief when he read in the tabloids that his wife had run off with another man, and was grateful that the *Times* did not consider it newsworthy.

Nor is it easy to comprehend why the novels of John O'Hara, concerned as they are with the shams and heartbreak of middle-class morality, may be appropriately reviewed on page one of the *Times Book Review* while any resemblance to the conduct of his characters in real life would be regarded as largely out-of-bounds for the news columns.

A newspaper, it has been said so often, is the first draft of history; but it can also provide, at its best, the first draft—or at least the raw material—of plays and novels and, in doing so, reveal a good deal more about its time than a dry chronicle of politics and economics.

I am puzzled when it is argued that it is especially inappropriate for a liberal newspaper to exhibit any interest in those stories usually associated with tabloid journalism, as if there were a peculiar incompatibility between liberal politics and matters of passion. This is almost like saying that the less we know about the interior of people's lives, the more expertly will we draft codes of conduct for their public behavior.

What is wrong, I repeat, with much of tabloid reporting is not that it dwells on the privacies of human conflict, but that it is too often either romantic or vulgar, simple-minded or cliché-ridden, and thereby wholly unrevealing when it pretends to be most revelatory. But that is quite a different thing from the studied refusal of some newspapers to confront what used to be called the facts of life, and to dismiss as unprintable the kind of story that will eventually form the plot of a Tennessee Williams play.

One of the misfortunes of the press is that its techniques have been so conventionalized that it is often uncongenial to writing talent; the sob-sister is often sent on the novelist's errand; stories are too often identifiable as Form A or Form B because rewrite men and desk men lack the inquisitiveness and audacity to defy the rules. Partly for those reasons, partly because the economics of the craft make it increasingly difficult to interest or retain the ablest young writers, there are embarrassing gaucheries committed every hour of every day in the name of "human interest." But organized dehumanization is not the answer. Ernie Pyle's war coverage

will be remembered when most war books have been remain-
dered, because he left politics and strategy to the others and
tried to write of war as it was seen by the lonely, morose
and baffled foot-soldier. In larger terms there must be moments, at least, when any newspaper shifts its camera from
the record of great personages, meaningful events and high
society to the gray quarters where the drama of most existence is enacted. In the old story, it is said that if some saga of
violent sensuality slips furtively into the *Times,* it is identified as sociology, whereas in lesser journals it is dismissed as
sex. Whatever the label may be, I simply suggest that a decade
capable of accepting the Kinsey reports as a record of our
manners and morals should be prepared to find some of the
findings documented in its daily paper.

More and more we are becoming a nation of "one-news-
paper" cities; where the proprietorship is unusually conscientious and dedicated, the result may be temporarily
salutary, but in the long run the condition is unhealthy;
only infrequently are the heirs the newspapermen their
fathers were. As the successions occur, the paper may increasingly become a commercial property quite divorced from its
earlier tradition. Barry Bingham and Sevellon Brown, Jr., are
bright examples of men who have taken their inheritances
seriously; too often, however, newspapers are simply handed
down to men and women who are concerned only with the
monthly balance sheets. In the absence of any competition
enterprises conducted in that spirit are likely to be drab and
uninspired.

The most conspicuous newspaper expansion in the present
period is that of the Newhouse chain, administered on the
frank premise that the owner's concern lies not with the con-

tent of his properties but with the returns at the box office; the only common denominator of each of the papers acquired by the Newhouse interests is that they are commercial triumphs. In a contracting industry any form of expansion probably is to be welcomed, but little daring or innovation is likely to be born of this approach.

Where is the resurgence to come from? Once or twice in every decade a Marshall Field III or a Dorothy Schiff may emerge to start afresh, but these are increasingly rare events. While the combination of inherited wealth and congenital liberalism is an isolated and lucky recurrence, it hardly seems to be the fashion of the day.

The one great untapped resource of sponsorship for a newspaper renascence would, at first glance, appear to be the organized labor movement. Time and again the leaders of labor have cried out against the distortions and infamies of "the kept press" and often their indictment is supported by strong evidence. The answer, one would imagine, would be a daily labor newspaper, perhaps published in a key industrial center like Detroit with local "replates" issued in other major union territories. There is nothing mechanically or fiscally impossible about such a venture, I am convinced, but there are many reasons why the idea has been rejected each time that it has been advanced.

Perhaps the most obvious is that the labor movement is not one movement but many, led by very disparate men whose intolerance for each other sometimes exceeds their impatience with those whom they regard as their common enemies. An enterprise of this kind would require a subordination of personal vanities and vendettas hard to conceive at this or any foreseeable moment. One need only look at samples of the labor press—the separate weeklies published by individual international unions—to recognize the unhappy pressures under which most labor editors toil, the sacred cows they are obliged to venerate, the ideological tightropes they must walk. Such papers are "house organs," and the head of the house is customarily accorded obsequious worship.

The launching of a labor daily would certainly entail union subsidization for a prolonged trial period; one can think of few labor statesmen who would be prepared to authorize the use of funds for a paper which failed to immortalize them or peered critically at their infirmities. Moreover, within the merged labor federation there are many varieties of political man, ranging from some of the old-line spirits of the Carpenters Union to such liberal mavericks as Walter Reuther. The editor who sought to please or placate such opposites might soon find himself longing for the comparative quiet of the Hearst enterprises.

Perhaps the largest hope for a new press start lies in a revivified political liberalism. The Democratic Party, divided as it is now, could hardly sponsor a national daily without running into constant argument with itself. But a liberal political movement—whether it be called ADA or by some other initials, or whether it represented a Democratic Party freed of its most conservative elements—might well provide the general auspices under which such a venture could be promoted.

Of one thing I am certain: there is no shortage of talent for new enterprises in liberal journalism. The conservative press—magazines and newspapers alike—is crowded with men, young and middle-aged, who would be happier in a different home, but for whom the area of choice is now acutely limited. Madison Avenue harbors others who still occasionally dream of more creative endeavors than the promotion of toothpaste. But they grow older each year, and their standards of living rise while the economics of journalism becomes more restrictive. Here, as elsewhere, too many men are "beat"—and the ranks of the woebegone seem to multiply rather than diminish.

CHAPTER 9

Communists and Free Men

WHATEVER Mr. Khrushchev may say about our grandchildren, our children are more likely to grow up to be beat than Bolsheviks. It may take some time longer for the country to recognize that the American Communist movement is a feeble wreckage, incapable of any major recovery; too many men retain a vested interest in perpetuating the myth of Communist power in our own land. What, for example, would the editors of *Counterattack* do if they confessed to their subscribers that the Communist Party has been reduced to a battered, impotent sect?

John Gates, the former editor of the *Daily Worker,* who resigned in January of 1958, offered this portrait of Communist collapse in his *Story of an American Communist:*

The American Communist Party has failed, and has disintegrated. Less than 5000 members remain, of whom no more than a third pay dues, and few carry on meaningful activities. The average age level is past 50, and for a decade there has been no recruitment of young people or new members.

Our literature is full of the record of mischief and misadventure of the American Communists, and it seems scarcely

necessary to whip the broken beast again. It is often noticeable that one generation appears singularly incapable of
communicating its experience to another; perhaps that explains why the Communists were able to recuperate from
the disaster of the Nazi-Soviet Pact in 1939 and boast of some
75,000 members—and innumerable fellow travelers—in the
period immediately after the end of World War II. It is
almost inconceivable, however, that another comparable rehabilitation can occur. The wartime alliance with the Soviets
momentarily rescued the U.S. Communists from oblivion.
But the brutal Russian suppression of the Hungarian rebellion and the Khrushchev revelations about the terror of the
Stalin era finally shattered the Communist mystique. There
is no place in American political life for a movement committed to the doctrine of Kremlin infallibility. Perhaps we
shall even see the day when there is no place for politicians
who resurrect the domestic Communist nightmare because
they have nothing meaningful to say about anything else.

This investment in the local business of anti-Communism
has produced some astonishing footnotes to the mounting
evidence of Communist decay. The theory has been widely
and persistently advanced by no less a dignitary than FBI
Director Hoover and echoed by the House Un-American
Activities Committee that the Communist Party grows steadily more menacing as its membership declines. Each report
of new and wholesale defections evokes the comment that
the survivors constitute the "true, hard core of Bolshevik
fanatics" and that they have become more formidable because
the weak and the wavering are no longer around to inhibit
them. Curiously, that is exactly what Communist leader
William Z. Foster and his forlorn cohorts bluster to one
another each time they are confronted by the news that
another detachment of their riddled troops has left them.

The notion that Communist strength is somehow in direct proportion to Communist decline is nonsense, whether propounded by Mr. Hoover or Mr. Foster; only a kind of continuing national paranoia induces any substantial group of Americans to succumb to the hoax.

Indeed, one sometimes wonders whether even the shell of the Communist structure would survive if Mr. Hoover were to withdraw all his underground agents from its ranks. They must surely constitute an increasingly high proportion of the membership and provide the backbone of circulation for the party's weekly newspaper (the remnant of what was once the *Daily Worker*).

As far as America is concerned, the Communist game is up; how long can what has become the anti-Communist racket outlive that news?*

There was a time when the Communists could not be so glibly written off. It would be inexcusable naïveté in the revulsion against McCarthyism to pretend that there was never any ground for concern about the Communist enterprise. Once upon a time it commanded the allegiance of an important and strategic bloc of labor leaders, including men like Joe Curran of the Maritime Union and Mike Quill of the Transport Workers—both of whom long ago turned on their ex-comrades. During the era of the Nazi-Soviet Pact the Communist labor battalions successfully created disturbances in certain key industries. In the national election of 1948 there were early forecasts that the Communists might roll up a vote as high as five or even ten million for their Progressive Party "front," and thereby create world-wide delusions about America.

* For further documentation of the Communist collapse, see David A. Shannon's *The Decline of American Communism,* sponsored by the Fund for the Republic (New York, Harcourt, Brace and Co., 1959).

In the end, however, the Communists had once again managed to destroy the thing they pretended to love; their crude domination of the Wallace drive, their insistence on vulgar rationalizations of the Russian position, their mechanical reiteration of Soviet slogans broke the back of the campaign and left Wallace himself bitter and disenchanted, with about 1,100,000 votes.

And they never came back from that debacle. It might even be observed that, by the time Senator McCarthy stumbled upon the "Communist issue" in the year 1950, the Communists were already on the run—decimated in large part by the counteroffensive of liberal and labor forces in the battle of 1948.

Surely it is time that we abandoned the diversionary exercise of hunting Communists in our bedrooms and backyards and recognized that the serious areas of Communist advance lie beyond the water's edge. Obviously there is a continuing need for effective counterintelligence; there is no reason to believe the Russians have halted the practice of espionage, although there is some doubt whether the Communist Party any longer serves as a recruiting ground for such agents. In any case the techniques of public hysteria can contribute nothing but confusion to what should be the quiet process of counterintelligence.

If the American Communist Party can no longer be regarded as a serious intrusion, its fate may offer us some wisdom about the authentic challenge that Communism presents in the world. We too often talk and act as if all the troubles were on our side; as if the commissars truly represented some modern form of invincible political wizardry; as if, in short, despite all the noblest deeds of Western man, the Communist tyrants were the wave of the future.

To overestimate an adversary can be as foolish as to minimize him. The Communist empire has registered ominous gains in the years since World War II, but it has also suffered grave reversals. Perhaps the most important thing that has happened—and that will be remembered by historians long after the skirmishes have been forgotten—is the crumbling of the monolith once known as The Third International. A specter haunts the Communist world—the specter of heresy. In the long run the resourcefulness with which we nurture this heresy may shape the course of our century.

This effort will require some fundamental alterations in our national attitudes—at least insofar as these attitudes are truly reflected by the stereotypes which now govern so much thinking in journalism and in politics.

Back in 1947 I heard what proved to be the most prophetic comment on the course we ought to pursue in dealing with representatives of the individual nations that formed the Communist bloc. The words were spoken by Benjamin V. Cohen, the thoughtful, soft-voiced early New Dealer who was then acting as a member of the United States delegation to the United Nations. The cold war was on; one of the great questions confronting us was what our demeanor should be toward those Eastern European delegates whose sole function seemed to be to sneeze in sympathy when Mr. Stalin had a cold.

Cohen insisted it was wrong to treat them—the Poles, the Yugoslavs, the Hungarians and others—as if they were beyond redemption. We know, he said, that for the moment they will vote and orate in complete conformity with the Russian line, shift whenever the Russian quarterback tells them to do so; they will behave like infuriating robots. Nevertheless, Cohen argued, it was important for us to maintain lines of communication with them; to talk to them privately, and to listen even when they were reciting the current banalities of Soviet propaganda. As human beings, he said, we should "treat them as if they were independent," even though they were, for the time being, entirely submissive.

It was not a popular view. In the context of the times it almost sounded as if it betrayed an excessive innocence. Yet it was the view that ultimately prevailed on a larger scale in our relations with Marshal Tito, thereby precipitating the first great crack in the world Communist front and inciting a disaffection whose echoes are still almost universally heard. Dean Acheson and Mr. Truman refused to be stampeded into a head-on collision with Tito when American fliers were shot down over Yugoslavia; despite all the clamor for impetuous reprisals, they recognized that the stakes were too high for any indulgence of national vanity. The bridge to Tito remained open, and Stalin finally drove him to taking the first tentative steps across it.

We need not romanticize Tito's defection; as this is written his jails are still occupied by men like Milovan Djilas who dared to suggest that the real root of the Stalinist disaster could be found in the one-party state. Tito was not overnight transformed from rigid Bolshevik to humanist democrat, and there is no assurance he ever will be. But whatever reservations we properly retain about the internal order of things in Yugoslavia, Tito's rebellion unmistakably shook the Communist world. It provided some of the inspiration for the heroic Hungarian uprising which, despite its tragic terminus, has left permanent scars on the face of Soviet despotism. It helped to stir dissent in the Polish Communist domain. It increased the stresses within the dormant conscience of Communist man—a species whom we had assumed to have long ago lost all contact with idealism. The robots displayed a new, if faint, animation; they no longer nodded in military unison; some of them began to ask questions about the degradation which decades of iron Russian rule over the world Communist movement had wrought.

We still know very little about the internal conflicts of the Chinese Communists, partly because Mr. Dulles decreed so long ago that it would be inconsistent with the national interest for us to try to find out anything about the nature of life on the Chinese mainland. There have been recurrent intimations that the rigidities and oppressiveness of the Chinese Communist regime may ultimately exceed even the darkest days of the Stalin terror. If that should be the result, we may well ask ourselves whether the quarantine we imposed was any service to the Chinese people or to ourselves. Can we be sure there was never a moment when American contact with the Chinese—as with the Yugoslavs—might have affected the course of Chinese history? Were there no potentials of discontent to be explored? In excluding the Chinese from the discourse of nations, did we weaken the grip of the commissars—or did we simply bring out the worst in them?

It will be said that the elementary rules of morality made any other position intolerable. The Chinese Communists, like the Nazis, had too much blood on their hands; to deal with them would be to sanctify the orgy of murder and mayhem in which they consolidated their power. Yet those who make that point rarely accept the ultimate logic of their piety; they do not, for example, suggest that we boycott the United Nations so long as the Russians are around, nor do they shrink from the increasing intimacies of our relationships with General Franco. On these levels they pride themselves on being "realists."

But the first rule of realism was stated long ago by Whittaker Chambers: "Every Communist is a prospective ex-Communist." It is here that the parallel between the Nazi and Communist empires loses its deadliness. Certainly the Communists can point to a record of blood-letting that rivals the Hitler horrors. But the commissar has clung to the delusion that all the wretched inhumanity of Communist man to man is a means to a great end; the Nazi proclaimed the glory of gore for its own sake.

Can we hope that men so steeped in the sadism and violence of Communist struggles for power retain any real contact with the better impulses that may have initially impelled them into Communism? Let us assume that at least some of them were animated by genuine visions of an egalitarian tomorrow when they first rallied around the red flag; after all that has happened to soil that dream, one might surmise that only the crazed and the craven can have remained loyal to the god that failed.

Yet the evidence is that men can emerge from the Communist movement after twenty years or more and exhibit a startling comprehension of standards that they had presumably banished from their minds long ago. In that connection I found the case of John Gates more fascinating than many more lucid and lurid Communist memoirs. He wrote his story for the *Post,* and I came to know him fairly well during that period.

Gates, as noted earlier, had been editor of the *Daily Worker* until his resignation from the Communist Party on January 10, 1958. He was forty-four at the time; he had been a Communist since he was seventeen, and a Communist "functionary" for most of the years of his life.

To the best of my knowledge and recollection, I had not known Gates personally during my own considerably briefer days in the Young Communist League (spring of 1934 to December of 1937). Yet I do recall that he was generally regarded as one of the "tough guys" in the YCL leadership, a man noticeably impatient with doubters, and zealous in his hunt for heresy. I knew that he subsequently served as a "political commissar" in the International Brigade during the Spanish Civil War; when word began to trickle back of the loathsome excesses committed by the Communist legions against their suspect Socialist and Trotskyist allies, I had some image of Gates as a man entirely capable of treating his friends as ruthlessly as his enemies.

We did not meet till many years later. In 1950 he and I were invited to debate at Sarah Lawrence College. In his own memoir Gates offers this account of the evening:

Dr. Harold Taylor, head of the college, acted as moderator. The subject of the debate was the Smith Act. I knew that Wechsler was an ardent civil libertarian and opposed the law, but while I devoted my talk to the Smith Act, Wechsler stated his position against the statute in a couple of minutes and spent most of his time on what was wrong with communism. I was indignant at these unfair debating tactics, as I felt them to be, but was nevertheless placed on the defensive.

One point which Wechsler made stuck in my craw. He said that one thing which he objected to most strenuously about Communists was that we were so certain and cocksure about everything that we never entertained any doubts. I responded by saying that doubt was the hallmark of liberals and led to paralysis of action, while Communists made up their mind and acted. Although I disagreed vigorously with Wechsler, his argument wounded me and I was never able to get it out of my mind. I thought about it again and again as the years passed, especially as events occurred which finally led me to understand what he was driving at.

Gates's reference to "doubt" was based on a quotation I had borrowed from Jennie Lee, the wife of Aneurin Bevan and herself a lifelong Socialist; I had told the students of once hearing her say that "the advantage the Communists have over the rest of us is that they do not respect the principle of doubt." She had gone on to point out that a reasonable skepticism about the validity of one's own beliefs did not necessarily entail passivity; it did deprive us of the comfortable assurance of ultimate victory—or salvation—that most dogmas give to their flocks. I had also asked Gates to indicate any single occasion when he had publicly dissented from any Russian policy. He was obliged to respond that he could not recall any moment of such unhappiness.

I bring all this up now because it is somewhat germane to the larger argument advanced here. It did not occur to me as I left Sarah Lawrence that evening that anything I had said might have been heard and thereafter recalled by this implacable veteran of American Bolshevism. And I remember being oppressed by the problem of the time. Most of those in the audience had probably been about six years old when the Nazi-Soviet Pact was signed; could any reference to the event give these young women a true glimpse of what it had been like to be twenty-four when that news arrived?

It was about seven years later that Gates approached me, through Joseph Starobin, an old friend and one-time associate in the YCL, and told me that he was about to leave the Communist Party. There had been some public advance notices of his decision; for Gates, as for some others who had stayed in the Communist setup almost as long, the Russian suppression of the Hungarian rebellion had finally destroyed the faith already shaken by Khrushchev's indictment of Stalin.

The "principle of doubt" had finally caught up with him.

During the preparation of his articles Gates and I had several long talks. He was like a man groping toward a door after a long slumber, rubbing his eyes as the faint light filtered through the window. Not too much earlier he had served a prison term as one of the defendants in the Smith Act prosecutions. Now he was emerging from an even longer incarceration. Just as he had found it difficult to eat rich food after a long prison diet, he approached this new freedom hesitantly and awkwardly.

There were still ugly truths about Communist history that he was reluctant to accept; there were probably also dreary episodes of Communist behavior which he preferred to forget. Because his articles did not have the full flavor of the "I confess" school of journalism, there were hardened characters who questioned the legitimacy of his defection. The Congressional investigating committees at once made it clear that he could prove the authenticity of his conversion only by promptly testifying before them, revealing all secrets and naming all names that he knew, and providing appropriate ornamentation wherever possible.

Thus the so-called experts on Communism once again proved how little they knew—or cared—about the real nature of the Communist experience. I have often wondered how many men have remained Communists long after "doubt" assailed them simply because they were fearful of being subjected to the pressures of the Congressional confessional, and because they felt there would really be no honorable place for them to go once they got out.

What matters most in the Gates story is what it says about even the hardest core of Communism, not merely in the USA, but in areas where the Communists still retain power or prestige. After twenty-seven years of dedicated duty to totalitarianism, Gates still detected meaning in the concept of freedom, human dignity and other words so often discounted by the commissars as "bourgeois" virtues. The years of brain-washing had not banished all vestiges of the humanity that sent him to Ohio to organize the bedraggled relief clients of 1932.

It had been a long journey—too long, some will say. It is not for me to pass judgment on that point. What is important for us to consider is how many other men in how many other places may yet seek a similar escape route if there remains a light in the democratic window.

PART III

MEN

AND MYTHS

CHAPTER 10

McCarthy and the

Aftermath

IT HAD been apparent from the bulletins throughout the day that Senator Joseph Raymond McCarthy was dying. In the city room there was—as there is always with respect to noted men in mortal agony—morbid speculation about whether he would favor the morning or the afternoon papers with his last big story. When I left the office our press-run was over and the final word had not yet come; when I arrived home half an hour later the news that he was dead was waiting for me.

I write subjectively about these moments because a day or two earlier one of McCarthy's newspaper worshipers had written that the Senator's liberal critics were "praying" for his death. The remark was as vulgar as it was unperceptive. Even if one were sufficiently lacking in humanity to pray for the death of the father of any small child, there could hardly have been any relevance in the exercise. For, though Joe McCarthy was not buried until May 7, 1957, his political life had ended long before. By the time of his admission to Bethesda Naval Hospital for his last losing struggle, he was a lonely, bitter, beaten man; he had been for many months.

And so the news of his passing evoked curiously personal rather than political reflections. It had been four years, almost to the day, that I had seen him last, and in the role of witness—or defendant—before the Senate tribunal over which he presided. That springtime of 1953 was a season of McCarthy's glory. Although I refused to concede him immortality, I would surely have hesitated to predict that his reign would last little more than another year. To many the words of Yeats seemed entirely contemporary:

> Things fall apart; the centre cannot hold.
> Mere anarchy is loosed upon the world.
> The blood-dimmed tide is loosed.
> The best lack all conviction, while the worst
> Are full of passionate intensity.

This was the season when the President of the United States remained aloofly neutral, when, except for stalwart figures like Herbert Lehman, William Benton and a handful of others, the basic law of political survival was avoidance of public argument with Joe McCarthy; when Roy Cohn was deemed one of the young men most likely to succeed in the American future; when the Wall Street Post of the American Legion was presenting McCarthy its Bill of Rights Gold Medal; when the voice of Elmer Davis sounded like an appeal from the American underground; when countless Americans were pushed around by McCarthy and his men with only scattered dissents from the American press; when for each unbowed John Oakes of the *Times* or Irving Dilliard of the *Post-Dispatch*, there were twenty editorial writers who felt it prudent either to salute McCarthy's services to the republic or write of less controversial matters.

Now, on the night of McCarthy's death, it all seemed very

long ago. Far from feeling any elation, I had a curious sense that I can only describe as a dreary anticlimax. For one thing, I had felt from my first encounter with him that McCarthy was not an unlikable man. Indeed, back in 1953, when the passions of the period still ran high and one might have been tempted to picture him as the classic villain of all political drama, I wrote of the committee hearing:

Throughout the interrogation the grand inquisitor was by turns truculent, contemptuous and bland. Yet I rarely had any feeling of personal animosity. He acted like the gangster in the B-movie who faces the unpleasant necessity of rubbing out someone who has gotten in his way; he would really like the victim to feel that there is nothing personal about it and that he rather regrets the exorbitant demands of duty. At no time did I have the feeling that I was confronted by a fanatic. McCarthy is a poker player, not a zealot . . . I think he is one of the least passionate demagogues I have ever encountered. I am certain that he would have been happy to shake my hand and forget the whole thing if I had merely indicated that I had misjudged him and was prepared henceforth to write kinder things about him.

I resort to the embarrassing device of quoting my own words lest my account of my reaction to McCarthy's death seem a retroactive genuflection to a fallen warrior. I do not propose that we erect any memorials to him. But now, as in the time of his glory, I often feel a sharper contempt for the able-bodied, full-grown men in politics and the press who bowed to him, pampered him and fled from him than I do for the crazy mixed-up man who was Joe McCarthy.

I hope this is in no way construed as intimating that it required any special valor for the editor of a liberal newspaper to invoke McCarthy's wrath. I have often observed that an editor needs no great inner fortitude to express the courage of his publisher's convictions, and from the start of the McCarthy madness there was no question about the attitude of the *Post*'s publisher. There were a few others in the same camp; but it was a painfully small contingent, and not until McCarthy had set the stage for his own disaster did any considerable body of newspaper opinion begin to make itself heard. One need not exaggerate the power of the press to suggest that there might have been a greater display of virility in public life if there had been fewer eunuchs at the typewriters.

McCarthy had certain genuine talents. He shrewdly exploited the readiness of most of the press to accept one-day sensations, especially in the realm of "anti-Communism," to publish the fraud on page one and let the facts try to fight their way into print at a later date. Being amoral, he was never inhibited by even the limited respect for truth that governs the activities of most men. He was not a Fascist; he was not a man disposed to any systematic ideology; had he come of political age in the depression-shadowed '30's, he might have chosen the left side of the street. He craved sensation for its own sake, and beneath the mask of furious righteousness that he wore, one could almost see the faintly cynical smile, as if he were continually fascinated by Barnum's ancient discovery.

McCarthy's essential frivolousness gave him large advantages in combat with more serious souls. As they groped to ascertain the precise measure of falsehood in his continuing book of nonrevelations, he would leap to a new theme; the discrediting of an earlier exposure was buried in the excitement created by the new one. He did not pause to quibble, or suffer any torment of self-doubt. He simply operated on the principle that the show must and would go on and on and on.

He was not superman; he was nourished more by the weakness of those who should have resolutely challenged

him—most notably Dwight D. Eisenhower—than by any mys-
terious resources. There must have been many moments
when he shook with laughter over the conduct of those he
was harassing; surely he must have enjoyed Mr. Eisenhower's
austere refusal to "indulge in personalities," the craven formula devised early at the White House for the preservation
of internal Republican peace and quiet.

In death, as in life, he brought out the worst in men;
seldom has the republic witnessed a more ghastly spectacle
than the obsequious funeral service conducted for McCarthy
in the same Senate chamber where he had been censured
three years before. There were, of course, men who liked
him and who might properly have desired to participate in
a farewell to him; but both the rhetoric and the ritual of
the Senate performance were the final indecency of the
McCarthy era. For over the whole assemblage hung the sense
that there might yet be some political mileage in McCarthyism, that he was somehow the embodiment of "the Catholic
vote," and, in deference to that sentiment, all was forgiven,
Joe. Certainly the sights and sounds on that day would have
affirmed McCarthy's conviction that every man has his racket,
and that in public affairs there is no possible connection
between what men say and what they believe.

Actually the ceremony merely underlined the moral corruption which had infested the Senate in most of its dealings
with McCarthy. The censure vote itself was not addressed
to most of the great issues. It was a punishment inflicted
belatedly for violation of the "rules of the club"; in the end
it was based, not on what McCarthy had done to many ordinary Americans, and to the countenance of a free nation,
but on his lack of reverence for the personnel and protocol
of the Senate. He was convicted not of being a bully but of
being a boor.

The suddenness of McCarthy's political death was nevertheless a remarkable phenomenon. It might have been the inspiration for the song: "He was a big man yesterday, but boy you ought to see him now." Why was the descent so swift and so catastrophic? In 1953 most of his prospective foes were mute, hollow men, looking furtively over their shoulders when they found themselves guilty of a spontaneous anti-McCarthy utterance. By the end of 1954 his political obituaries were being written by even the most timid journalists.

I should like to believe that the outcome was a happy ending for a saga of democracy; that McCarthy's own disdain for the basic decencies of a free society plunged him into the war with General Zwicker that ended in defeat and disgrace; and that the television coverage of what became known as the Army-McCarthy hearings finally brought the meaning of McCarthyism into the homes of millions of hitherto inattentive and apathetic Americans.

Certainly there is some validity in this theory. One of the most memorable moments in the country's political annals was the brief, wounded cry of outrage uttered by Joseph Welch after McCarthy had suddenly and savagely attacked the political sins of a young lawyer who was utterly unrelated to the proceedings. It was then that Welch turned on him:

> Until this moment, Senator, I think I had never really gauged your cruelty or your recklessness . . . If it were in my power to forgive you for your reckless cruelty, I would do so. I like to think that I am a gentle man, but your forgiveness will have to come from someone other than me.

I was watching the hearings at that moment with a group of newspaper colleagues; there was a startled silence and then an outburst of cheers. It was as if we had all been waiting very long for someone to speak in exactly such terms, not in the usual language of political cliché but in affirmation of those elementary instincts that had come to seem old-fashioned during the McCarthy heyday. And this is what Welch had done. Somehow he had said better than all the editorials and the public orations what needed to be said: that in the conflict with Communism we are doomed if we abandon the standards of personal conduct that ostensibly differentiate us from the commissars. It was as if a gentleman and a scholar had told off the street-corner bully who had held a town in terror, and by that single act cleared much of the American air.

Deep as is our debt to Mr. Welch, it would be an excess of romanticism to describe this single episode as the fall of Joe McCarthy. Probably it hastened the end, and let it be a lesson to the disenchanted of the role that good men can play in history. What Welch spoke for was nothing more nor less than human kindness—the topics of our sermons, the cherished of our virtues. He had done what so few of McCarthy's colleagues had ever dared to do—proclaimed in a public place that protection of an obscure American life from random assault was as much the concern of our politics as of our police.

McCarthy was partly, of course, both the creature and victim of history. His life span as a major national demagogue roughly corresponds with that of the Korean war. It was just two months before that war began that he delivered his notorious Wheeling address in which he first claimed to hold in his hand documents proving that subversion was rampant in the State Department; it was sixteen months after the Korean truce that he found himself the target of the Senate's censure resolution. One might persuasively argue that, without the rancor and frustration stirred by the dead-lock in Korea, McCarthy might never have achieved more than the marginal eminence won by such predecessors in the field as Martin Dies.

But neither Mr. Welch's gallant thrust nor the pattern of events constitute the whole story of McCarthy's decline, and of the speed with which he went from Capitol Hill to political skid row. I am inclined to agree with Richard Rovere that the secret of McCarthy's ultimate failure also lay in the cynicism which gave him so many temporary advantages. "His talents as a demagogue were great," ob-served Rovere, "but he lacked the most necessary and awe-some of demagogic gifts—a belief in the sacredness of his own mission." In the times of triumph, McCarthy did not need any body of belief to sustain him; the rewards were in the headlines won by head-hunting, in the continuing tur-moil he stirred, in the exuberance acquired from the spec-tacles of weakness around him.

Once he got into trouble, however, it became obvious that, in the old phrase, he just couldn't take it. Men who care deeply about something—call them fanatics when they disagree with us, or men of deeply rational conviction when we like the sound of their words—can endure long interludes of adversity, of deprivation, of prison or exile. But McCarthy was the leader of a crusade for which he didn't give a damn except insofar as it advanced the cause of Joe McCarthy; when the reversals began, he panicked, and the panic pro-duced blatant blunders. With the legend of his invincibility shattered, he lost his poise and his confidence. He could not retain any hope of ultimate vindication because it had never occurred to him that there was permanence in the life of any idea.

In an earlier time McCarthy might not have given Welch

the cue which enabled him to steal the production. But the deterioration had begun; and now he faced an adversary who refused to play dead. McCarthy had hurt many lives just as he tried to destroy the young man whom Welch defended. But to commit an act of such brutal dimensions under the spotlight of the television cameras was a desperate deed. Perhaps it can only be said for those who never contested his earlier excesses that they helped to make him the man he was on that fateful day.

In any case the discovery that he could no longer get away with this form of murder plainly shook him. Illness and frustration became his daily companions; no doubt a large body of modern medical knowledge will contend that the two were deeply interrelated. There remained at his side a small battalion of devoted believers; but how could they give him new passion for an adventure in which success alone mattered? From the moment that the reversal occurred, McCarthy was truly through. If he could no longer believe in his own future—and the signs were ominous—he could believe in nothing. It is not true in politics that they never come back; a defeated candidate for the Vice-Presidency in 1920 lived to serve more than three terms as president. But such comebacks require tenacity, will, resolution.

The extraordinary fact about the man who frightened so much of America and the world for so long is that, in the final assessment, he turned out to be a weak man; neither his head nor heart were equal to the trial of defeat. This was McCarthy's tragedy and the U.S.A.'s lucky break.

Indeed, what is most fascinating in the work of McCarthy's apologists is the lack of revelation about the nature of the man. They have built a shrine to a cardboard figure; they tell us little or nothing about what he was really like. I suspect that the omission is a form of acknowledgment.

Shortly after the publication of Rovere's critical study of McCarthy, he and I participated in a symposium on the book with L. Brent Bozell (co-author with William Buckley of the most comprehensive defense of McCarthy). Buckley was also present, and both men argued that Rovere had deeply wronged McCarthy. But when I suggested to the believers that there would be little profit in rehearsing our old arguments and perhaps some enlightenment in a discussion of McCarthy as a man, neither rose to the invitation. I was not proposing any crude invasion of privacy; I was urging them to give us a glimpse of a human being for whom they presumably had both affection and reverence. But the debate remained wholly impersonal. I could not escape the feeling that they either knew the man too well, or not at all, and that what they knew was inconsistent with the simplistic legend of dauntless super-patriot they had helped to create.

The rewriting of history is a popular American sport. With respect to the era of McCarthyism that process has already begun, and some intellectuals are no less guilty than some politicians of pretending that the nightmare never really occurred. Naturally this point is argued with greatest vigor by those who were preoccupied with other matters when the battle was raging.

Again let me not be misunderstood. It was much easier for some of us to participate in the argument, because of the nature of our work, than it was for others. Neither Elmer Davis nor Ed Murrow was fired for saying what other men preferred to think in private; Mr. Lehman left the U.S. Senate by his own decision; Herblock's drawing board was never taken away from him. On the other hand there were undoubtedly circumstances in which men had to choose between survival and speech—or believed that they did—and chose to live to fight another day. My point is not to prolong recrimination about those who were missing in action but to dispute the comfortable notion that nothing serious was going on.

It may take a long time to obtain a full and accurate appraisal of the damage that was done and the scars that endure. That it was considerable I have no doubt; that it will be remembered in the history books as one of America's darkest ages seems equally clear to me; that it could happen again—given some grave turn in world affairs—is a possibility not lightly to be dismissed.

The human damage inflicted is too easily forgotten as memory recedes. Again I refer not to those of us who were able to fight back, but to those obscure and anonymous citizens—at Fort Monmouth and other places—whose lives were so rudely interrupted by McCarthy's intrusion, and whose ultimate return to society took so long in so many cases.

But this, of course, was not the total cost to the nation. A volume could be written on the demoralization and disruption that McCarthy wrought in both the foreign policy and the foreign service of the United States. One would want to know how many times discussions of high policy, and execution of low policy, were affected by whispered and nervous speculation as to what McCarthy might say or do if . . . In crucial areas that warranted constant re-examination, such as our relations with Chiang, McCarthy helped to tongue-tie a nation. What makes all this so preposterous is not that a single Senator was able to exercise a kind of continuing veto power on any new initiatives in foreign affairs. It is that the Senator who exercised this power happened to be, by all available evidence, a man singularly

uninformed and even essentially uninterested in this whole
domain.

I have often felt that throughout McCarthy's reign, and
even in the years of the aftermath, a major aspect of the
peril created by his tantrums was often lost. It was not merely
that innocent lives were cruelly wrecked, and that in free
society we must live by the principle, in Judge Hand's words:
"Risk for risk, for myself I had rather take my chance that
some traitors will escape detection than spread abroad a
spirit of general suspicion and distrust, which accepts rumor
and gossip in place of undismayed and unintimidated inquiry." It was not merely that we dishonored ourselves in
the community of nations; our own self-respect is still more
crucial than what others think of us. Nor was it simply that
we found ourselves proceeding from the legitimate process
of excluding Communists from vital government positions
to the institution of a vast man-hunt embracing janitors and
cleaning women, and using the McCarthy challenge to justify
the need for continuing the absurdity. (What government official did not at some time or other rationalize his
excesses of vigilance by reminding his aides that McCarthy
would "get them" if they didn't watch out?) All that was
bad enough. What was obscured was an affirmative concept—
that freedom of speech and association is not merely one of
the glories of our way of existence, but a fundamental protection and stimulant.

"The real evil of suppression," Morris Raphael Cohen
once wrote, "is not that it is ineffective but that it deprives
the society that practices it of the opportunity to enlarge
its vision of the good life and to realize its best potentialities
through processes of peaceful change.

"The importance of encouraging rather than suppressing
diversity extends beyond the realm of discourse. All fields of

life are impoverished by the monistic mania for uniformity which serves as the background for the ridicule and persecution of that which is peculiar."

There was admittedly a tendency in some places abroad to overstate the case against us during McCarthy's golden years. He did not ever achieve the full power and glory of which he dreamed; he hounded and paralyzed the State Department at critical moments, but there always remained pockets of resistance to him; the President resisted his more audacious proposals for unilateral military action, which the Senator himself could hardly have taken very seriously. And in most universities the business of learning went on as usual.

Yet if European reports of the death of the republic proved to be exaggerated, there is no warrant for accepting the new theory that the McCarthy era was a trivial, almost comic interlude in the happy American story. Much of government and of Congress was reduced to a condition of servitude for more than three years; in a time of great international storm, the land of liberty found itself engaged in defacing its own image to the world, and its leaders absorbed in a kind of guerrilla warfare—when they fought at all—with a political racketeer.

There are those who concede that the unpleasantness did occur but insist that, since the consequences weren't fatal, no serious reckoning needs to be made. After all, they argue, the fact that McCarthy's political life was so brief dramatizes the fundamental vitality of the country; wasn't it best to "give him enough rope" since he never had time to hang too many of us, and finally helped to destroy himself? This view is especially popular among the political fans of Democratic leader Lyndon Johnson, who managed to escape any harsh political encounters with McCarthy until the whole Senate pack was ready to move in for the kill. It will probably also be advanced by the admirers of Senator John F. Kennedy, who has apparently not yet detected any irony in his determination to write a book called *Profiles in Courage* which ignored the crisis of courage created by the McCarthy thrust.

It is perhaps unfair to single out any of those legislators most conspicuously missing in action; there were so few present. The flight crossed all party and ideological lines, and that is why, even in retrospect, there is so ominous a quality about it. By the prevailing standards, Adlai Stevenson was a "premature anti-McCarthyite"; his early speeches remain among the brighter public papers of the era, and immediately evoked lamentations from some of the bigger Democratic leaders. By and large elder and younger statesmen alike joined the flight, praying that the plague would pass. Hardly a political figure in the land seemed to possess sufficient faith in freedom to believe that the country would one day—even in our lifetimes—revere those of its leaders who dared to resist bully-boy.

On almost every side there was a failure of national character; as one examines the long lists of presidential hopefuls for 1960, it must be said that nearly all of them approach the tryouts with equally undistinguished records on the McCarthy front. But let those of us deemed eggheads not impose too severe a verdict on the politicos; "judge not lest ye be judged . . ." I vividly recall a large meeting sponsored by the American Committee for Cultural and Intellectual Freedom back in the winter of 1953. The subject was the McCarthy attack. A variety of orations was delivered, including an impassioned defense of McCarthy by Max Eastman, still engaged in penitence for his early Marxist days and more McCarthyite than McCarthy in spirit. At the end of the meeting a few of us proposed the adoption of an anti-Mc-

Carthy resolution but cooler heads prevailed; it was agreed, for reasons that still elude me, that this public gathering was an inappropriate place for such a declaration, and that the matter should be referred to the executive committee for study. It was with such diligent discretion that even a large assemblage of intellectuals moved in that time. Let it be added that the executive committee finally did adopt a resolution along those lines, but the lack of spontaneity of the larger meeting seems to me more characteristic of the period than the declaration finally given painful birth in committee.

I have reserved for the last of this chapter the point most relevant to the larger inquiry; but I assume that much of it is implicit in what I have already written. To what degree has the climate of youthful opinion—or lack of it—been shaped by the McCarthy experience? Has the generation that grew up during the long McCarthy night suffered some traumatic shock, of which the symptoms are speechlessness in all conversations affecting public questions? Can the vogue of nonparticipant be traced to the inquisitions so extensively conducted during the last decade—inquisitions begun, let it be remembered again, by Attorney General Tom Clark in the time of President Truman, and extended far beyond any reasonable protection of "sensitive" government areas.

Any unqualifiedly affirmative answer would be absurd. We cannot afford the luxury of ascribing all our national hollowness to Mr. McCarthy or to that more general condition called McCarthyism. It might even be said that, to some of the more sophisticated set, the moral collapse of national political leadership under the McCarthy gun may have been far more demoralizing than any sense of personal danger induced by his conduct.

But I would also quarrel again with those who glibly

write off the impact of the period on those who were coming
to consciousness in it. For one thing, McCarthy proclaimed
the proposition that anything you strongly believed now
might be held against you two decades later unless you were
astute enough to keep the belief to yourself. The course of
prudence was clear. Possibly more important, McCarthy created the national sense that we are all being watched; that
one never knows how even an isolated action or remark may
some day be weighed by a prospective employer. Paranoia
is infectious. Much of the disease that McCarthy brought
to the land lay not in the reality that he achieved but in
the expectations that he created; and there was enough reality to give some substance to the dreariest dread.

It was at the height of the McCarthy tumult that Elmer
Davis wrote:

It is quite true that 'tis man's perdition to be safe when for the
truth he ought to die—or, as the phrase is more likely to translate
itself in these times, when for the truth he ought to lose his job,
with small chance of getting another. But it is, emotionally, if
not ethically, a somewhat different matter to tell a young man
with a wife and children whom he is barely able to support on
his salary that for the truth, his wife and children ought to starve
too. And that is a situation that increasingly comes up in the
present drive, Congressional and local, against freedom of
thought—particularly in the schools and colleges where above all
freedom of thought must be preserved. Professors and teachers in
schools and colleges are tempted to pull in their horns, to say
nothing at all; otherwise their students, or their students' parents,
might report them to the American Legion—as has happened—
and any deviation from the norm of reactionary thinking will be
regarded as subversion. With the result also, as Mrs. Roosevelt
reported after her nation-wide travels in the winter of 1953, that
the young people who are just coming up and see what is hap-

pening begin to be afraid to think and afraid to act, for fear that something they may say or do now will be dug up and thrown at them twenty years later and ruin their careers . . . A despotism might be able to stand this loss of heart, though I doubt it; but a republic whose young people are in that state of mind is on its way downhill.

Above all things Elmer Davis was a responsible man. He was not disposed to derogate his own country without what he regarded as good and sufficient cause; he would have derived no semblance of satisfaction from the knowledge—as some Communist fellow travelers so often seemed to do —that the United States was being reduced to absurdity in the world. And so what he wrote in the midsummer madness of 1953 may have larger journalistic validity than the retrospective reveries of those who now assure themselves that there was no conflict of consequence taking place at the time.

This alone, I repeat, is not what made young men seem "beat" or "silent" or singularly lacking in desire for any form of participation in the political engagements of our time. Possibly what happened was a combination of many things: of the security afforded by the Eisenhower myth, of the insecurity stirred by the McCarthy mythology, of the general sense that it was safer to play it safe. Always we have to remember that only a fragment of the population ever really risks involvement. Justice Holmes said "man is born to act. To act is to affirm the worth of an end, and to persist in affirming the worth of an end is to make an ideal." But few in any time live by that credo; in life, as at the stadium, the throng in the grandstand is always infinitely larger than the company of players. Yet for that activist fraction of a generation, no matter how small, the thing that McCarthy taught was that it was better to keep your eyes bleary and your mouth shut. None of us may ever know the whole cost of that lesson so crudely taught.

I am sure there will be professors of both English and French at many universities who will say this is all an overstatement because they never changed their scripts during the difficult period under discussion. The question that remains, of course, is whether anything they were saying might ever have invited any argument in either language.

At any rate this we do know: thousands of young Americans grew up in a time of abject national cowardice; a time when political leaders almost unanimously fled from combat with a man they secretly identified as an unscrupulous demagogue; a time when hollow men were everywhere. Perhaps there was only a dim awareness in many minds of the extent of the capitulation; yet it is hard to believe that no skeptics were born out of the debacle.

And the age of timidity is still with us in many places; men are still being imprisoned for invoking the First Amendment in response to inquiries that deal not with their acts but with their beliefs and associations.

It is perhaps the drabbest footnote to the era that in the widely celebrated novel called *Advise and Consent*, written by a Washington newspaperman named Allen Drury, there is a character whose reckless demagogy and contempt for truth are unmistakably drawn from the life of Joseph Mc-Carthy. But the novel offers several amendments to history; in Drury's version McCarthy becomes a man named Fred Ackerman, an irresponsible leftist engaged in a cynical, fraudulent defense of a character who is a composite of Alger Hiss, David Lilienthal, Henry Wallace and Dean Acheson.

I suppose literary license is limitless but it seems painful that a new generation of Americans may so misread the events of the last decade, and that so few men challenged this odd revision of such recent happenings. One might even call this the Senator's final triumph, and the peak of his grand deception. It is rather odd that a novel should have been his posthumous forum.

CHAPTER 11

Life of a Salesman

IT MIGHT be said of Richard Milhous Nixon that he has converted lack of conviction into a pious faith. Al Capp, challenged in a radio interview to explain his distaste for Nixon, was asked whether he had truly studied the man's words. He responded quickly: "Yes, I've heard him—on every side of every question." In the autumn of 1958 James Reston reported that the Vice-President had reached a strange, puzzling crossroad in life. While "those who know Nixon best" believe he is "closer to the liberal wing of the Republican Party" than to the Old Guard, it was the conservative faction that deemed him its spiritual leader and remained the chief bulwark of his presidential aspirations.

But while "those who know him best" were detecting varieties of liberal impulse in the inner Nixon, he had just completed a frenzied—and largely unsuccessful—national effort to save the political necks of a long series of reactionary Republican candidates. In doing so he had reverted to the key tenets of Republican orthodoxy and to the gutter tactics of "the old Nixon." Now, in the aftermath of that campaign, Nixon was said to be solemnly weighing his future course. The question seemed to be reduced to this: "Which Dick

Nixon shall I be?" Should he take the high road or the low road to the Republican Convention of 1960?

The change of face is not unique in American politics. It is sometimes politely described as a change of pace. But Nixon, perhaps more than any other man on the political landscape, symbolizes the idea that ideas should never be permitted to stand in the way of private political advancement. There were differences in style and manner between Joe McCarthy and Nixon when they were sharing the stage, but the central unbelief was common to both of them. Nixon has exhibited greater ability to achieve totally cold-blooded detachment about the business of politics, and to shift gears overnight. Yet the essential absence of commitment always seems visible.

Not that Nixon is totally incapable of creating the illusion of sincerity, even of dedication. The trouble is that he has seemed equally "sincere" when reciting the platitudes of Republican McKinleyism as when playing the role of modern man. His political double life may finally catch up with him, but little that has occurred in the Nixon saga to date offers much comfort for the view that honesty is the best policy in the jungle of office-seeking.

Indeed, it can be argued that many chapters in the Nixon success story to date seem to illustrate the reverse principle. In the Congressional election of 1946 and the national election of 1950 he defeated Jerry Voorhis and Helen Gahagan Douglas, two of the ablest members of the liberal bloc in Congress. He did so by campaigns that he describes as "rocking, rolling," the Nixon euphemism for systematic misrepresentation of issues and personal slander. It was, of course, the case of Alger Hiss that elevated him from California eminence to national renown; in this affair his persistence and perseverance were unmistakable and nothing partisans

of Hiss have produced in subsequent years convinces me
that Nixon was the architect of an injustice. But neither
would his labors in such a case appear sufficient to qualify
him for the Vice-Presidency in any era except one of national
incoherence.

He achieved that post at the age of thirty-nine, incontestably a distinguished coup for the young-man-in-a-hurry
from Whittier and additional proof of the carelessness with
which we produce our Vice-Presidents. He survived the
ordeal of the 1952 campaign in which it was disclosed that
he had been the beneficiary of an $18,000 fund raised by
wealthy California businessmen for the care and feeding of
Mr. Nixon. Small children may not remember but few
adults can forget the television soap opera he performed,
with the aid of his wife and his dog, to keep his place on
the ticket after that exposure.

On the surface the facts seemed damning enough, and
there was nothing Nixon could do to change the facts. He
had accepted the special fund without shame and with full
knowledge that much of the legislation on which he would
vote affected the interests of his patrons. Yet Nixon was
seemingly successful in persuading many Americans that he
was an innocent man wrongly accused, and he had his wife's
cloth coat to prove it. In retrospect what seems extraordinary
about the episode is not that Nixon accepted the fund but
that he could exhibit so profound a belief that no impropriety was involved. Clearly he was more persuasive than
Charles Van Doren.

Nixon's orations that year and in the Congressional campaigns of 1954 prompted Adlai Stevenson to describe him as
a "white-collar McCarthy."

It was in 1954 that Nixon engaged in the notorious exercise that became known as "the numbers game." At one

juncture, he boasted that the Eisenhower Administration's security program had ousted "thousands" of "Communists, fellow travelers and security risks" employed during the Truman era. As Philip Potter of the *Baltimore Sun* has noted,* a Senate inquiry later revealed that the Eisenhower Administration had itself hired 40 percent of the employes it listed as risks; that 90 percent of the cases counted in the security statistics had actually been separated through routine Civil Service procedures, rather than under the Eisenhower program, and about five percent of the "ousted" were still federally employed, having simply shifted jobs.

But by the end of '54 McCarthy's star had fallen; Nixon himself had turned his back on the broken god. Not too long afterward there emerged the first intimations that a "new Nixon" was in the making, and that he would bear little surface resemblance to the old.

The calculation was clear enough; the fever of McCarthyism was largely spent, and a man whose political career was so largely identified with it could hardly envisage himself as the next President of the United States. With the President's first heart attack, the ascendancy of Nixon had suddenly loomed as a real possibility—either by immediate succession or through the processes of the 1956 elections. As the uncertainty over Mr. Eisenhower's plans grew, it became increasingly imperative that the boy politician be hastily transformed into a statesman.

One would like to believe that a great reincarnation occurred; that, at forty-two, Richard Nixon became a man and that the awful responsibilities which might become his at any moment gave him a new vision of history. Certain outward manifestations supported this view. He was reliably reported to be studying hard in the fields of foreign policy

* See *Candidates 1960,* ed. Eric Sevareid (New York, Basic Books, 1959).

and economics. He was picking the brains of some of the eggheads whom he had hitherto treated as suspicious characters. His speeches acquired what was described as "a higher tone." He even conversed with labor leaders. Steadily, from a variety of Washington journalists who had obviously been granted private audiences, there came "authoritative" dispatches pronouncing the birth of the second Richard Nixon.

The most comprehensive account came from Stewart Alsop, writing in the *Saturday Evening Post*. Alsop, it was explained, had been privileged to spend several hours with Mr. Nixon, and his article was accompanied by a series of direct questions and answers in which Nixon purported to tell what spirits moved him.

The article was a readable and in some ways illuminating report. It suggested, for example, that a talk with Nixon could be quite interesting; knowing Alsop's sensitivity to the state of boredom, this was high tribute. Unhappily, Alsop was not permitted to provide any specific samples of the livelier lines. He pictured Nixon as a rather shy, introverted man who found the public routines of politics rather burdensome. Nixon is obviously not a back-slapper, and his baby-kissing is unquestionably awkward. Indeed, the Alsop report indicated a certain pathos about Nixon's political career. For he is plainly a man consumed with a passion for high office—or even low—and he began running for it successfully in high school. Yet he seems remote and ill at ease in the human give-and-take that is so much a part of political activity.

With all its human, and inhuman, touches, the portrait of Nixon that emerged was less than inspirational. It did full justice to his solemnity; it exploded the myth that he is some sort of personal demon; it indicated a certain curiosity of mind and temper. All that was missing, one might say, was any evidence that Mr. Nixon had any important ideas to communicate, any bold new visions about the world or the country, any major mission in life except the acquisition of power, any serious degree of humility about the spectacle he had made of himself on the way up, any profound convictions by which he fastidiously lived.

The most important, significant words in the production are spoken by Nixon himself. Asked to discuss "the role of politician in our kind of society," he replied:

You've got to be a politician before you can become a states-man—a lot of people have said that before me. In my own case, when I first came to Washington in 1946, I was a bit naïve about public service, I suppose, a kind of dragon slayer. Then, when I got here I was soon disillusioned. You know, you come to Washington, you have great ideas, and there you are in the committees or on the floor of the House, and you have an inability to implement your ideas. You see men who are—well, I don't want to sound pious but—less well motivated, and who know how to play the game, and they accomplish what they want. Then there are the Don Quixotes, the idealists—like Jerry Voorhis, my first opponent, a man of very high ideals—who never accomplish anything much.

You've got to learn how to play the game, if you're going to implement your ideas, and you've got to fight it out. You often find you've got to take half a loaf when you want the whole loaf. The best example of a combination of idealist and practical politician is Theodore Roosevelt. When he wanted to get something done he would compromise all over the place, if necessary. Read the autobiography of Bob La Follette. La Follette throws off on T.R. . . . says he's not a true liberal because he compromised too much. But who accomplished more, Roosevelt or La Follette?

There are many intriguing sounds in this soliloquy. Nixon's ode to Jerry Voorhis—"a man of very high ideals"—

is a curious footnote to his campaign of 1946 in which he drove Voorhis out of public life by fraudulently picturing him as a dangerous radical and front-man for subversion; the tribute would be more impressive if mingled with even a parenthesis of remorse about the operation which so crudely disposed of this worthy opponent.

Equally eye-catching is Nixon's remembrance of his early Washington days when he visualized himself as "dragon slayer" bursting with "great ideas." Alas, he concedes, the dragons were never slain, the ideas remained suppressed, and so he became a practical man. But what were the dragons he dreamed of routing, what were the high thoughts that were driven underground? We are never told.

The record shows that in his early years in Congress Nixon voted with the right wing of the Republican Party on nearly all major matters. He was a faithful spokesman for conservative business interests in domestic affairs, he was often, though not always, aligned with the isolationist faction in matters of foreign policy. It was presumably this record of solidity that earned him the business community's most tangible expression of gratitude—the $18,000 fund. One longs to know what the "real Nixon" was thinking while compiling this voting record, or is this retrospect fantasy woven by the "new Nixon" to prove there was never an "old Nixon"? It is all rather baffling.

Finally, of course, there is the pledge of allegiance to the flag of realpolitik—"you've got to learn how to play the game, if you're going to implement your ideas . . ." Ah, how often one has heard those words from politicians explaining why it is the right thing to do the wrong thing. Like all political bromides, this is not a total untruth; but neither is it the whole truth. And when a political dignitary uses such words, one must also ask what ideas are to be "implemented" and when, if ever, the "implementing" will begin. For, by his own standards, certainly Nixon has "learned to play the game." And now that he has done so, what great ideas has he brought to fruition? Indeed, what are his ideas? Though we explore many pages, we get few answers. In Alsop's view Nixon is "instinctively conservative" but not a doctrinaire rightist; in foreign affairs he has increasingly recognized the economic and political nature of the Communist thrust; he certainly cannot be equated with the know-nothings who persist in proclaiming that military solutions alone can save us even though we all be destroyed in the process.

In Earl Mazo's affectionate biography of Nixon, we learn that Nixon always considered the issue of school desegregation a deeply moral as well as legal matter. But Nixon somehow avoided any warm public expression of this viewpoint in the long interval when the President was refusing to invoke any moral sanctions against the forces resisting integration.

Any summary of Nixon's ideas adds up to very little and remains palpably subject to change without notice. Nixon is capable of behaving like a perfect gentleman and scholar. He demonstrated that on his journey to Britain in 1958. He understood that, when in Britain, sound as if you read the London *Times,* if not the Manchester *Guardian,* especially if you are a presidential aspirant. The major foreign policy speech that he delivered sounded as if he had been reading Adlai Stevenson. He had set out, in short, to convince a suspicious, critical audience that all the obscene things it had read and heard about him were the distortions of irresponsible journalists and cunning Communists. He responded sympathetically to Britain's dread of atomic war; he displayed his mature understanding of the virtues of British colonial history, too often, as he saw it, obscured by its acknowledged vices; he left at home any vulgar assaults on the iniquities of the welfare state, such as those he had been delivering only a few weeks earlier in the Congressional campaign. He acquired everything but an Oxford accent.

By all accounts his journey was a vast success in exactly the terms in which he had conceived it. No longer, it seemed, would the British press write in apprehensive tones of the possible accession of Nixon to the Presidency; no longer would his candidacy be deemed a threat to the Anglo-American alliance. From almost every section of British newspaperdom came declarations of esteem for the Nixon they had never known. Randolph Churchill exclaimed gleefully that Nixon's expedition had finally taught the British public that earlier images of him were the handiwork of "crypto-Communists and fellow travelers."

In view of the vaunted political sophistication of the British press, Nixon's achievement was large. Coming in the aftermath of the loss of prestige he had suffered in the 1958 Congressional race, it was almost as stunning an exhibition of resilience as his Checkers speech of 1952.

As I read the British press notices I thought back to a Republican rally Nixon had addressed in New York during the final phase of the 1956 campaign. It was what he would call a "rocking, rolling" address. I was at the press table when he delivered it, lured there by all that had been printed earlier in the campaign about the "new Nixon." There was nothing new that night; this was a familiar old voice, proclaiming that a Democratic victory would mean ADA rule of the country, decrying the alleged tendency of Democrats to practice socialism, invoking all the old bogeymen that have frightened elderly Republican ladies ever since Herbert Hoover left Washington.

Watching him that night I was more fascinated by the style than the substance of his speech. Nixon still retains all the basic techniques taught to high-school debating teams. And, as in the case of the high-school debater delivering a text, there seems to be no necessary connection between the speaker and the words. One never knows at a high-school debate whether the young orator really favors the proposition assigned to him, or gives a genuine damn about it; he is engaged in scoring points to win a contest. And though I have acknowledged earlier that Nixon is apparently able to communicate a surface of "sincerity" to many audiences, I found no such quality in the air that night. Perhaps that was because that was not "the real" Nixon. How will we ever know?

It will be said by Nixon's admirers that, like many other men, he too must compromise in order to get ahead; but let him be his own president and then we will really see the man that has been so long hidden behind all these masks. The difficulty with that theory—and it applies to other men, too—is that, unless there is a core of demonstrated belief, it can be used to justify perpetual lack of motion or emotion. Once a man becomes president, he must begin thinking about his second term; what better justification for "compromise"? And then, when finally the second term is won, it is too late; he is already on his way to becoming a lame duck.

Although I have written most here about what seems to me the absence of Nixon's ideas, I suspect there is another deficiency that explains why so many people, regardless of race, color or creed, find him an unattractive political leader. The lack is embodied in the song: "You Gotta Have Heart." But perhaps all this reflects a more deep-seated prejudice toward a man who was known as a "model boy" in college. On a platform Mr. Nixon always reminds me of those whom we used to describe as teacher's pets, and I never believed much good would come of the breed. This is admittedly a private petulance based on surface view.

What makes Nixon so tantalizing a figure is that he has gone so far with what seems to be so little, and with an inconsistency so palpable as to raise doubt as to whether there is anything that might be called the "real" Nixon, new or old. It is perhaps the greatest monument to his artifice that he could be the subject of a campaign biography described as an "objective" portrait; who else would have authorized a study that gave us a glimpse of the two faces of Mr. Nixon and permit it to be advertised as a true account?

Perhaps more than anything else, the Nixon story is the climactic triumph of two-headedness in our political system. Here is the man who rises to public eminence over the debacle of Alger Hiss and achieves his second great glory when he journeys to Moscow to consort with the leaders of Russian Communism. Here is the man whose sole claim to political distinction was as the anti-Muscovite abruptly transformed into the exponent and champion of negotiation with the devil himself. And two months after his journey his stock in the Gallup Presidential poll had risen nearly ten percent.

In Moscow, as everywhere, he was still the young debater; almost overnight the conflict of our century seemed to be reduced to a platform in an obscure high-school auditorium, and there was never a great moment. Nixon persistently misstated the issue as a clash between capitalism and Communism, rather than between freedom and despotism; most American editorial writers assured him he had scored all the points, and he returned as the triumphant peacemaker. Soon afterward, however, he was mending his right-wing fences; he was appearing before the Veterans of Foreign Wars, exhorting the delegates to support maximum preparedness, as they always had before.

There was an interesting sequel to Nixon's adventure as missionary to Moscow. It had obviously created consternation among his old adherents; but by the time Nikita Khrushchev had arrived for his American junket Senator Barry Goldwater, the lonesome right end of the U.S. Senate, felt able to offer some reassurance. In a Chicago speech to a conservative assemblage he announced:

"Let me tell you, Nixon is a conservative. He was as shocked as you were at the invitation to Khrushchev to come to this country . . . I can only relate what the Vice-President said to me. He said he was greatly surprised. He had no knowledge of the invitation. He was surprised and disappointed the invitation had been made."

In Moscow some weeks earlier, when he got the news of the Eisenhower bid to Khrushchev, Nixon had publicly endorsed the move. But he never disputed Senator Goldwater's version of his later remarks. On the basis of the record, it is reasonable to assume that all the reports were true, and that Mr. Nixon had once again managed to brace himself squarely on both sides of the fence.

One may still ask whether Mr. Nixon's schizophrenia is more acute than that of most leading political men. Perhaps it is not; perhaps what differentiates him is the utter mirthlessness, lack of self-consciousness and clear-eyed earnestness which he brings to his double role.

He is, one might say, the embodiment of the line about the old judge—"often wrong but never in doubt." In 1956 he denounced Adlai Stevenson's call for suspension of nuclear tests as "catastrophic nonsense . . . the height of irresponsibility" and "the most dangerous theme of the campaign." In 1959, when his immediate adversary, Nelson Rockefeller, urged the resumption of tests, Nixon swiftly announced that anybody who recommended this course "didn't know the facts."

He is the avowed believer in organized spontaneity. "A good off-the-cuff informal speech," he once remarked, "takes more preparation than a speech you read, and the candidate must realize that he can't just get up there and talk off-the-cuff without having spent hours in preparation." This comment was made in the course of an address to the Radio and Television Executives Society in which he emphasized the importance of "seeming sincere" and described the prepared unprepared speech as a valuable device in the simulation of straightforwardness.

The other side of this strategy, Nixon once explained to Ralph de Toledano, is the avoidance of emotion. "The only time to lose your temper in politics is when it is deliberate," he observed. Other political men are guilty of artifice and humbug; but few men have made so calculated a science of it. Probably only a man lacking in deep belief can treat politics as a continuing sport, and perhaps such a man will be especially bitter when his hollowness is challenged. Such an occasion was Nixon's appearance before a press conference of college editors at Cornell. After the television time had expired, some of the inquisitive editors continued to grill him and their inquiries suggested that he had been evasive. Finally Nixon whispered to one of his associates: "Get me away from these little monsters." He is said to have gone to his room and "blown his stack."*

One might say of Nixon that he is the most complete "beatnik" on the political landscape. In him the absence of conviction and commitment is most fully expressed, and yet he is perfectly capable of saying, as he did in 1959, that the

* See *Candidates 1960*, ed. Eric Sevareid.

great test facing America is the discovery and affirmation of our beliefs as a nation:

Around the world, in every nation, the representatives of communism are true believers like Mr. Khrushchev—working overtime for the victory of communism in every non-Communist nation.

Our case is infinitely better. But men who are true believers cannot be matched by men who believe in nothing or, worse still, who do not know what they believe.*

There is every reason to assume that he wore the countenance of sincerity when he said it.

* Speech at the University of Chicago Law School, Oct. 5, 1959.

CHAPTER 12

Struggle for a Soul

ACCORDING to the yardstick set by Henry Luce's political writers and echoed widely in the American press, Hubert Horatio Humphrey is obsolete at forty-eight. Despite certain unhappy and largely unsuccessful attempts to harmonize himself with the "practical men," he is forever reverting to ancient liberal gospel. Just when he is about to be taken seriously by Arthur Krock and other pundits whose true test of a man is his divorcement from the "ADA liberals," Humphrey finds himself, in *Time*'s words, abandoning the "moderate role," throwing away the carefully prepared script of discretion and becoming "a wildcat liberal." He thereby eliminates himself from the consideration of those who presume to know that in the year 1960 such language belongs to the past.

The experts who discounted Humphrey's candidacy before it began may well be right; his may be a wholly lost cause doomed by all the realistic circumstances of politics; amid all the uncertainties and unpredictables of our national contests, perhaps the one sure thing is that Humphrey is a sure loser. It is not my purpose to quarrel with the analysts, so many of whom (including myself) so pitilessly deluded Mr.

Dewey in 1948 by assuring him that he was immune to the accidents of the political road. Regardless of whether Humphrey proves to be a serious figure at the Democratic Convention, the nature of his predicament warrants examination. It has a good deal of bearing on the role of liberals in politics, and on the impact of politics on liberals. And the questions presented go far beyond the triumphs and traumas of this Presidential year.

At the start some personal preconceptions must be recorded. I have known Humphrey for more than twelve years—from the time he became one of the first officers of Americans for Democratic Action and thereby paved the way for much of the political derision to which he has been subjected in large areas of the press. At the time he assumed this post he was the mayor of Minneapolis, little known beyond the borders of the Twin Cities, and his chief tub-thumper was Jim Loeb, then executive secretary of ADA and a man hopelessly addicted to searching the hinterlands for new liberal talent, much as if he were a scout for the always hopeful Washington Senators.

I hesitate to augment Humphrey's excessive political burdens by any exaggerated claim of proximity to him. I have seen him on and off during the intervening years at conventions, dinners and occasional hotel-room seances attended by small groups of unreconstructed and sometimes oddly shaped eggheads. I have written editorials denouncing as well as praising him, and there have undoubtedly been moments when he was tempted to ask me whether I had ever been elected dog catcher anywhere, and how I presumed to offer so much self-righteous counsel from the privileged sanctuary of a nonelective editorial office in New York.

All this is by way of preface to challenging certain myths about Humphrey—myths nimbly nourished by conservative journalists but accepted in some degree by other citizens who have no essential quarrel with him. The most serious of these myths is that Humphrey is a man who talks a great deal but cares very little, who embraces many issues, with passion for none: a sort of political nymphomaniac forever professing lifelong devotion to a momentary cause and then leaping into another ideological bed at the first beckoning. This is what is meant, I assume, when some refer to him as the "Democratic Nixon."

I would be hard-pressed to argue that Humphrey does not talk a great deal, and about many things, and occasionally without adequate provocation, and sometimes without full appreciation that the physical resources of his listeners are unequal to his own. No one knows this better than Humphrey, I suspect, and in his defense I can only testify that he possesses both humility and humor when taunted about the compulsive verbosity from which he suffers. A couple of years ago, in introducing him as the keynote speaker at an ADA banquet on a Saturday evening in Washington, I remarked that I assumed he was familiar with the Sunday law which forbade any speaker to begin an inning after 11:59 P.M. He responded quite amiably to this admonition, but I subsequently learned that a number of his close associates were offended by my observation. They felt that, since I was familiar with his rhetorical ailment, a decent respect for the troubles of a friend should have compelled me to avoid mention of the problem in public. When I learned of the disquiet I had caused, I wrote Humphrey assuring him of my continued esteem, and his response was both wiser and wittier than I deserved.

Admittedly he does talk too much, and he does find it hard to remain aloof from any current combat. Yet it seems entertaining that any editorial writer or commentator should find this ground for condemning him. One might almost say that his crime in this regard is the daily offense that all of us commit on the editorial pages and on the air; on how many occasions has any of us announced we will maintain silence on a big topic because we have not yet gained access to sufficient independent knowledge?

Questioned about his varied involvements, he exclaimed on one occasion: "You people write that I talk on every subject. I do—I *like* every subject. I can't help it—it's just glands." This injudicious comment may not answer all the critics, but it seems to me a human condition preferable to the widespread characteristics of elusiveness and disengagement.

Humphrey is a self-conscious man with an inferiority complex about Eastern intellectuals; indeed, one irony of his story is that he is so often berated for pretending to know all the answers when in actuality he is so acutely aware of the complexity of the matters before him.

Despite all his apparent gregariousness, he is a lonely figure in the political world. Perhaps more than any other man, he is torn between earnest conviction and the councils of caution and discretion. It is a dilemma rendered no more cheerful by those who would "remake" him as a middle-of-the-road character mistakenly depicted as an extremist. Those who try to do so do him an injustice. He is not Richard Nixon, and he cannot become a "new man" tailored to momentary political circumstance.

Perhaps there ought to be something like Verbosity Anonymous, whose members, when tempted to speak out on matters of which they know not, resolve instead to call each other up and take a drink. But the truth about Humphrey is that he makes an inordinate effort to learn much about many things; the record of his public utterances is probably scarred by fewer malapropisms and misstatements than that of any of us who offer daily published opinions; the range of his interests is genuinely wide, remarkably earnest and not easily matched.

But there is a more important truth about him, which I again divulge with full awareness of the hazard to his candidacy. He is a man with deep, instinctive ties to the liberal movement. He is likely to be at his best addressing a rally of the Liberal Party in New York, a caucus of Americans for Democratic Action or a convention of the Automobile Workers Union or the National Association for the Advancement of Colored People. It is in such settings that he is the despair of those advisors who feel he must alter his image to "win acceptance" as a Democratic product. He is clearly most exuberant and most at home with himself when he tells such an assemblage that the cause of civil rights is a fighting concern, and that he will not compromise it in the quest for higher office. At such moments, even though he may have broken the organization's record for verbal longevity, there is an authentic excitement in the hall, as if the audience is refreshed by contact with someone who cares and who will not revise his text in a different setting tomorrow.

On another level, Humphrey has worked long, hard, conscientiously and with little public forensics on the issue of disarmament. For a long time he received pathetically few press notices for these endeavors. But what is noteworthy about the effort is that he brings to it a mingled sophistication and idealism equaled by few men in public affairs. He brings to it few illusions about the Russians but a large awareness of the desperate stakes for which mankind is playing. We would not, I venture to say, have allowed the Kremlin to seize the propaganda initiative in this domain so often if he had been in a position to dictate the Administration's public attitudes and pronouncements.

What I have written so far may have the sound of a campaign speech; I hasten to add that it is far from the whole story. I have put it in affirmative, even affectionate terms because I am alternately fascinated and dismayed by the hostility of the press which Humphrey has encountered, by the derogatory murmurings I have heard in some liberal places, and by what seem to me the excessively critical standards by which he is widely judged.

My point is that Humphrey's crucial difficulties do not reflect lack of heart, intelligence or imagination; these are qualities with which he is almost uniquely blessed. He is not the creature of opinion polls; his judgments are not disconnected from his instincts. If it be said that he is an ambitious man, let someone cite the one who truly is not. None of us who shuns politics as a personal endeavor can render any pious verdict. Any very active participant in life—whether he be actor, general, journalist or baseball player—probably possesses an internal chemistry that makes him prefer a certain amount of tumult to what he regards as the monotonous quietude. The saving quality in a political man is conscience, an admission of his own frailty, a sense of guilt and doubt each time that he consciously says what he does not believe, or does what he knows to be wrong. I can think of no public figure—with the possible exception of Adlai Stevenson—who experiences emotions as complicated as Humphrey does when he finds himself playing the game in defiance of his own loyalties and beliefs.

In a sense the astonishing thing is that Humphrey's inner torments often seem so invisible to a society which has come in many places to picture Mr. Nixon as "sincere" if misguided.

The decisive difference between the two men is the matter of commitment. Anyone who examines Humphrey's history can find a core of belief and conviction to which he harshly deems himself answerable even when he departs from it; he is never less congenial with himself than when he is behaving like "the organization man."

Yet it is the very intensity of the pain to which he is subjected—he asked for it, of course—that stirs the largest inquiries about the falsity of our political system. Consider some crises in his personal chronicle.

In 1948 he emerged at the Democratic National Convention as the leader of the insurgent drive for a full-scale civil rights program. It is hardly a secret any longer that the effort was conceived at a disorganized, chaotic caucus at a fraternity house in Philadelphia where the ADA mavericks were gathered, and that there were great pressures on Humphrey from his more worldly-wise advisors to shun the effort. He was thirty-seven at the time; he was presumably a young man going places; and when, for whatever reason, he made his decision to stage this insurrection, there were many who assumed this was his farewell performance. Humphrey himself lived through a night of cruel uncertainty, and as late as 5:30 A.M. was still unsure whether he would risk the wrath of the "pros." I do not know at what moment he made the final decision, but it was surely his biggest moment. When he reached his decision it must have been with a sense that he preferred to be right rather than victorious; the odds were overwhelmingly against him. Then one of those rare political miracles occurred; the "regulars" who had dictated compromise on civil rights were beaten on the floor of a convention where such unlimited democracy is never supposed to prevail; Mr. Truman (one of those who had supported the compromise course) thereupon embraced the rebellion, used it to enormous advantage in his campaign and acted as if he had been with Humphrey from the start.

Hubert Humphrey, in any case, was now a national figure.

Now comes the summer of 1954. The McCarthy frenzy is not yet exhausted; Humphrey—despite all his earlier effort in leading ADA's offensive against Communist penetration of the liberal movement—is among those being hounded and harassed with the cry of "softness on Communism." And so, in violation of everything he professed to believe about the meaning of civil liberties in America, about the scope of the McCarthy fraud, about the distorted attempt to make domestic Communism seem the large peril when the great tests were being fought on foreign battlefields, Humphrey abruptly becomes the sponsor of a "Communist-control-bill" more extreme than anything McCarthy had proposed. In retrospect he says of that episode:

"It wasn't one of the things Humphrey is proudest of. It grew out of my frustration and anger over the way the Republicans were using the Communist issue. I just decided to do something about it. It got the issue out of Congressional committees and into the courts. And it saved the life of two Democratic Senators."*

The rationalization was weak, and delivered weakly, with the unfortunate reference to a third person named Humphrey, and with, I guess, a faint, embarrassed smile. All that can be said for it is that other men might have tried more stridently to justify the inexcusable. But it was not to be the last exercise in what might either be called self-deception or self-betrayal.

In advance of the 1956 convention Humphrey was plainly given reason to believe he had a chance for the Vice-Presidential nomination. The price he had to pay, it seems clear, was abstention from any bellicose role in the civil rights debate. Somehow the Southern contingent had to be persuaded that he was no longer the man they had known in 1948, but an

* See *Candidates 1960*, ed. Eric Sevareid.

older, more sensitive spirit who recognized that no new Southern day could be ushered in overnight. In the preceding Senatorial session Humphrey had established closer personal as well as political bonds with Senate Leader Lyndon Johnson. He had avoided excessive militance on the civil rights issue; there were even those who said he now held some credentials as a member of the Senate "club," and was no longer viewed as the hot-head, the irreconcilable, the intransigent.

So Humphrey spent many hours in his hotel room at Chicago, evading any pugnacious intervention in the convention's affairs, accepting if not relishing the characterization of growing-older statesman which seemed a prerequisite to the call. The call never came, and Humphrey has never quite excused himself for awaiting it so cynically.

It may be said that I display excessive tolerance for Humphrey's failures and follies, when contrasted, for example, with my judgment of Senator Kennedy's silence in the McCarthy era. Perhaps I am partly moved to do so by the overwhelming evidence that Humphrey's mistakes are never lightly noted in the mass media—that he is almost continuously the subject of scrutiny more exacting than any other candidate must face. Whatever his sins, they never seem to be proportionately quite as large as his detractors insist. To put it bluntly, I think they suspect that he is an unredeemable liberal—and it is my suspicion that they are right.

A good deal of history is simplified in this recapitulation. But the essential simplification is valid, and remains operative now.

For Humphrey, partly because the intensity of his convictions has been abundantly demonstrated on a whole succession of issues, is the target of a struggle for his soul. On the one hand, as this is written, he is being urged anew to recognize that he can be a meaningful candidate only if he "lives down" his identification with the liberal bloc, if he creates the image of a reputable, responsible, regular fellow somewhat appalled by his own past fervors, and who is willing to wait patiently for the deadlock in which such assorted seers as Jake Arvey, Harry Truman, Carmine DeSapio, Lyndon Johnson, Dick Russell and other pillars of the backroom turn to him as their leader out of the convention wilderness.

This possibility seems to me as preposterous as it is demeaning. What gives the Humphrey candidacy any sense of excitement it may possess is that he happens to be—despite his misadventures—the most authentic liberal candidate in the Democratic household. He has, for example, been urged often and feverishly to turn his back on ADA; he has never done so, and I believe he would loathe himself in the morning if he did.

Humphrey often appears glib, cocky, wordy, wisecracking; these are the nervous faces of a man deeply troubled by the routines of politics and almost apprehensive about wearing too serious and insecure a countenance when he presents himself. He is the most extroverted introvert I have ever known.

But he is also a man caught in the web of deceit created by the falsity of our two-headed party system. More than any other man, he is being told that his lone hope for emergence from the scramble and the shambles is to pretend to be something other than he is, to become a "new" Humphrey on a scale never quite visualized by the "new" Nixon, to curb not merely the length of his speeches but the fire in his spirit and to prove that, in the era of the uncommitted man, he too can be above the battle, or, at least, missing in action.

In a way he is being asked to relieve the consciences of all other Democratic aspirants. If Humphrey can be persuaded to act as if the things in which he believes are generally regarded as "extremist doctrine" and that there is no future for a man who holds to such beliefs, then all other men must be equally forgiven for each of their abandonments of principle. After all, for better or worse, he is the candidate most plainly identified with the liberal tradition; if, in a time of compromise and vagueness, he is unwilling to rejoice in the liberal label, who is to challenge the instinctive compromiser? Alternatively, who can create greater discomfort for all his adversaries by refusing to play it safe?

Now that all this gratuitous counsel is given, let me add that it is in no sense offered as a formula for personal success. Conceivably, in our state of stalemate, only the adaptable man, unfettered by strong feeling and conviction and blessed with a flexible TV personality, can make the grade; perhaps there is no room at the top for the candidate who frankly proclaims himself a fighting advocate, who cuts through the sham of our present party structure and who demands clear debate on great issues. Humphrey has a vision of what America ought to be, and of the potential grandeur of its role in the world and, at his best, he acts and thinks in terms of that vision. I get no comparable sense about most of his competitors.

I do not offer Senator Humphrey as the next president of the United States; I offer him only as a decisive laboratory test of whether a liberal is doomed to defeat or self-destruction—or both—by the fraudulent party alignment under which we live. And if the answer is that he is a hopeless case, how long will he and men like him try to live within this stultifying framework?

CHAPTER 13

Thundershower on

the Right

ONE EVENING not too long ago I debated with William Buckley, Jr., in a Long Island community. It was neither the first nor the last time we have met on a platform; we have achieved something of the relationship of vaudeville performers. We also have, perhaps unhappily, a clear glimpse of each other's views, and our most earnest epigrams no longer come as a surprise; we are, it might be said, each other's straight man.

So perhaps we should have been prepared for what happened on the train taking us to Manhattan on that occasion. We were, as usual, returning together, somewhat wearied by the day's work as well as the evening's encounter. Under ordinary circumstances I think we would have exchanged pleasantries, complimented each other on anything new either one of us had said and settled down to the long voyage home.

But just a moment after the train had left the station a young lady—I guess she was about nineteen—suddenly appeared in the seat facing us (willing to ride backward for the confrontation) and abruptly announced: "Look, I came all the way from the Bronx because I can't decide which of you is right, and I still don't know the answer. I have a lot more questions."

And then, for the ensuing hour, she questioned us. I think Buckley will agree that neither of us was at his best; it really was quite late, and we had both talked for a long time. We both tried but, by the time we reached Pennsylvania Station, I had the sense that the deadlock remained unbroken.

For those who may have come in late, I should reintroduce Buckley. He is the editor of a magazine called *National Review*. He was graduated from Yale in 1950 and thereupon produced a volume called *God and Man at Yale,* a critical study of what he deemed the collectivist liberalism and/or atheistic materialism of the Yale faculty. He quickly emerged as the voice of American "young conservatism" and, in that posture, dedicated himself to the leadership of Senator Joseph McCarthy, whose deeds he immortalized in a volume that tried to explain far more skillfully than McCarthy could have done the essential virtues of the Senator's crusade.

As a debater Buckley is glib, erudite, alternately the perfect gentleman and the slugger, deferential and contemptuous, and rarely dull. If anyone detects a degree of warmth about someone with whom I passionately disagree on nearly all subjects confronting the republic, it is because I find it at least possible to join issue with him. I can best state the measure of our disagreement by noting that he regards the graduated income tax as an intolerable fetter on the natural rights of man.

Perhaps that is why a young woman would have bothered to undertake a train ride on the precarious Long Island Railroad to hear us argue. Whatever else might be said about our exchange, we could hardly be accused of repeating each other, or of blurring the areas of controversy.

At no point did either of us suggest, as is the fashion of modern debate, that there was not really much of a gulf between us, that we agreed more often than we disagreed and that one could find a neat "consensus" reconciling our views. In truth we are very far apart, and we do not attempt to deceive ourselves or our audiences on the point.

There is nothing particularly historic about these clashes. I cite them because they offer some counterpoint to the tame rhythm of modern political discussion in which the "moderates" of the Republican and Democratic parties grope cautiously for points of clear dispute, and in which the chairman inevitably ends the proceedings by pointing out that we are all really allied by the quest for common objectives divided only by minor shades of differing emphasis and quite as one in our resolute opposition to the Russian threat.

I am sure there are men of moderation in the audience who will say it is a good thing for the country that my quarrels with Buckley do not reflect the national political temper, and that we are a happier land because the issues are rarely drawn on the Congressional stage with such bellicose clarity. I do not know how the young lady from the Bronx finally appraised our dialogue; perhaps we made her a beatnik; but at the very least I am certain she sensed the ultimate and total divergence of our views, and that she could hardly have been uncertain as to which of us was which when the train pulled into the station.

I should hardly contend that Buckley represents any mass political formation in contemporary America. He finds the expediencies and compromises of right-wing Republicanism as offensive as I find the retreats and surrenders of liberal

Democrats. But to those who would neatly equate us as the rival "extremists" of politics I would reply that the matter of the income tax is really settled, while the matter of civil rights is not; and that much of Buckley's preoccupation with a return to a society whose premise is that what is good for General Motors is really good for the country is as unrealistic as it is wrong. I would further assert that it is a distortion of the banner of "conservatism" to preach in its name the abandonment of virtually all the social gains and reforms of the last two decades; indeed, this is a "radicalism" as sweeping and violent as anything embodied in the other-worldly recommendations of the Trotskyites and other surviving left-wing sects which still see redemption for all of us in a Marxian framework almost completely unrelated to the continent we inhabit.

What makes the Buckley movement interesting, it seems to me, is precisely the fact of its separation from the American reality. Certainly there are men in industry and commerce and finance who share Buckley's desire to repeal the New Deal, disband the United Nations and scrap almost every other faltering step we have made in the direction of social reform and world order since the time of Warren G. Harding. He has, let it be conceded, belatedly accepted the social security system—a symptom, perhaps, of advancing middle-aged mellowness. But there is not, in my view, any grave prospect that the Buckley legions will seriously alter the course of American history in our lifetimes, and those who proclaim their adherence to what they would call "the middle way"—placing, let us say, right-wing Buckleyism and ADA liberalism at polar extremes—are utterly misstating the political conflict of this period.

There may yet be resurgences of the kind of know-nothing reaction symbolized by Senator McCarthy and rationalized by Buckley; we are all at the mercy of the circumstances and accidents of world affairs. But this does not seem to me to be the large and likely choice. What is far more clearly drawn is the choice between do-littleism, represented with equal fervor by Dwight D. Eisenhower and Lyndon Johnson, and a revamped, revived progressivism that goes far beyond the dimensions of any existing political program, discarding the clichés of "economy," of "balanced budget," of inert, passive and lukewarm government which have become the non-battle cries of our time, and which make our shortcomings so apparent to a restless, hungry world.

Indeed, what makes an examination of the Buckley credo —and of its counterparts in such journals as *The Freeman* and in the writings of such amiable ex-liberals as John Chamberlain—relevant is the barrenness of the formulae offered. Liberalism has its bad days and listless hours; but, in contrast with the shallow reversions of so-called conservatism, it still retains the aspect of a fighting faith.

It must be admitted, of course, that there is a certain wry solace for any functioning liberal in a contemplation of the Buckley boys, and their more aged counterparts.

For liberals suffering from tired blood, dismayed by their failure to communicate with the new generation, doubting their own strength, saddened by the seeming treacheries of men who win elections under their banner, a contemplation of the condition of this breed of "conservatism" may provide some small tonic.

Some of our heroes may depart, not for a handful of silver but for a favorable press notice from Arthur Krock; others may become bogged down in the muddy terrain of what they deem realpolitik; the notion that all compromise and double talk are somehow sanctified because Franklin D. Roosevelt engaged in them gains prevalence. Granted all those things, some perspective may be restored by momentarily looking at the world as the rising young conservative sees it. Consider, for example, the manifesto of the Intercollegiate Society of Individualists, to which Buckley and his fortnightly, *National Review,* have dedicated so much effort:

"Socialism is a weed, a virulent one because it has long roots. In America its seed was implanted in the minds of our youth thirty, forty, fifty years ago.

"The weed cannot be rooted out; that's like trying to eradicate it by cutting off what appears above ground. Socialism will disappear only when the New Deal and Fair Deal generations shall have passed from the scene—and then only if the new minds that take over harbor an understanding and love for Freedom.

"It is the purpose of ISI to plant the idea of Freedom in the college mind, the mind that shall shape the America of the future . . ."

Here, indeed, is the full cry of political despair; not in our lifetimes shall the damage be undone; only our children may live to see the better day, and only if the process of revelation begins at once.

One turns, as I have indicated, to Buckley and his adherents for an examination of conservatism because, alas, it is almost they alone who hold aloft the flag and proudly bear the label. Like nervous liberals in politics who prefer to be known as "middle-of-the-roaders," few of those in public life who share Buckley's world view desire to be known as conservatives. The least modern Republican prefers to be identified as a champion of thrift, frugality, nationalism and, on some days of the week, is even likely to proclaim that he is the true liberal. Rare is the candidate who comes soliciting our favor as avowed, unashamed conservative. But Buckley does, and if, once upon a time quite long ago, it was possible to say that *New Republic* and *The Nation* were authentic influences on the thinking of political progressivism, so it may be said that Buckley and his cohorts provide the ideological framework for the right wing in U.S. politics and business.

Throughout his works Buckley has managed to confuse the economic doctrines of the National Association of Manufacturers with the certitudes of theology (although, by his criteria, many of the papal encyclicals on labor and social relations would have to be seen as evidence of the intrusion of fellow travelers into the higher echelons of the Vatican). In the heyday of McCarthy, Buckley was his emissary to the élite; he translated McCarthy's disorganized clatter into the patter of intellectuality just as, it might be said, he adeptly finds high social justification for every antisocial practice of the business community.

Richard Hofstadter, in pointing out that Buckley's self-identification of conservative is hardly precise, noted that Buckley and his men "although they believe themselves to be conservatives and usually employ the rhetoric of conservatism, show signs of a serious and restless dissatisfaction with American life, traditions and institutions." But whether they be known as conservatives or pseudo-conservatives or radicals of the right, there can be no mistaking the intensity of their suffering. Hofstadter observed that they are "opposed to almost everything that has happened in American politics" in the last twenty-five years—including the "practical conservatism of the Eisenhower Administration; they loathe "the very thought of Franklin D. Roosevelt." They are "disturbed deeply by American participation in the United Nations" which they see as an entirely sinister enterprise. On the one hand they see America as so weak that it is constantly on the verge of succumbing to internal subversion, but on the other so strong that it could run the world if it were not "betrayed" by its own. They are "the most bitter of all our citizens about our involvement in the wars of the past, but seem least concerned about avoiding the next one." While they profess their hatred for Soviet Communism, they often "show little interest in" and often oppose "such realistic measures as might actually strengthen the United States— vis-à-vis Russia"—especially the extension of economic aid to underdeveloped areas. They are more obsessed with the "domestic scene, where communism is weak, than with those areas of the world where it is really strong and threatening."

In the world as they see it, the ADA is the dominant if hidden power, the press is an instrument of the ADA ideologists, The Establishment is essentially shaped by the resolutions adopted at ADA conventions. The liberals, in short, have won all the decisive contests and have been remorselessly engaged in the consolidation of power, whether the occupant of the White House be Dwight D. Eisenhower or Harry Truman.

Viewed from a certain angle, there is ground for such lamentation. It seems inconceivable that in the foreseeable future any major movement to repeal the income tax or the social security laws will take root in American soil; there is no visible prospect that the Securities and Exchange Commission will be abolished. Alas for the Intercollegiate Society of Individualists, one does not even detect any clamor for the transfer of the Post Office to private hands, despite the wretchedness of the service in recent years.

The right-wing rebellion is largely a phenomenon of the last decade, achieving its importance primarily as a result of its identification with McCarthy's crusade and clearly losing a good deal of its momentum since his death. Yet it is not without interest, partly, as suggested before, because it provides some rationalization and research material for such activists as Senator Barry Goldwater and for nostalgic industrialists, and partly because it has created some animated support on some college campuses in a time when undergraduates are assertedly preoccupied with other things. And its emergence is some additional testimony to the fads created by the vacuum in politics.

In a sense the *National Review* has become something of a house organ for all the know-nothing groups which have heretofore lacked an urbane statement of their resentments and prejudices. Year after year the Daughters of the American Revolution have met in convention assembled to herald the Bricker Amendment as the last defense of American sovereignty; now, in lengthy essays, some of them written by glib ex-radicals, the Daughters can find out what the Bricker Amendment is and why they are really for it.

Not too long ago I found myself debating with Frank S. Meyer, one of the editors of the *Review*. It was a debate that covered many differences, but what made the evening more memorable than others was my recollection that I had last seen Meyer some twenty-five years ago when he was a member of the Young Communist League. He was the young man regarded at the time as one of the "promising theoreticians" of Communism because of his unmistakable gift for Marxist gab. On the occasion of our reunion, he was seriously advancing the thesis that free public education was one of the great blights of our society.

In the end the Buckley breed of conservatism proves to be contradictory and self-revealing. It remains committed to all the oppressive intolerances of McCarthyism, bulwarked by Buckley's own avowal that he has glimpsed final truth; simultaneously it trumpets the glories of business freedom as the only salvation for our "socialist-shadowed" society.

Having recited his critique of real and alleged liberal misdeeds in a volume called *Up from Liberalism,* Buckley proceeded to outline his affirmation: "What then *is* the indicated course of action? It is to maintain and where possible enhance the freedom of the individual to acquire property and dispose of that property in ways that he decides on."

Where "residual unemployment" exists, let us deal with it, he says, by "placing the political and humanitarian responsibility on the lowest feasible political unit." Let us above all avoid intervention from "the Washington office rooms where the oligarchs of The Affluent Society sit . . ."

And finally: "Is that a program? Call it a No-Program if you will but adopt it for your very own. I will not cede more power to the state. I will not willingly cede more power to anyone, not to the state, not to General Motors, not to the CIO. I will hoard my power like a miser, resisting every effort to drain it away from me.

"I will then use *my* power as *I* see fit. I mean to live my life as obedient man, but obedient to God, subservient to the wisdom of my ancestors; never to the authority of political truths arrived at yesterday at the voting booth. That is a program of sorts, isn't it?

"It is certainly program enough to keep conservatives busy, and liberals at bay. And the nation free."

But is it?

It may be contended that I have disputed my own view of Buckley's ultimate unimportance by this extended commentary. On that point I can only say, as I said at the start, that there is at least the pleasure in his works and words of discerning an unblurred position, unqualified by the usual reservations, reticences and retractions common to so much of our political speech. In a way I always found it more interesting to debate with an outright apologist for Senator

McCarthy than to quibble with those faint-hearted intellectuals who deplored McCarthy's assault but were forever finding reasons for evading direct combat with him. By the same token it is almost refreshing to argue with someone who would repeal the income tax rather than with that species of politician who is forever finding some elaborate justification for some obscure tax benefit for some favored area of business.

What is perhaps most important is that Buckley has managed to stir some spark of earnestness in some young men and women, not all of whom may necessarily be the beneficiaries of his tax program. I submit that his success—like that of the Communists two decades ago—is primarily a reflection of the general failure of the accredited political leadership to make the younger set take it seriously. Ah, but will they not be wiser if we just let them grow up? Is there not an impulse toward "extremism" in a certain fraction of any generation? Perhaps there is; but it is a harsh reflection on the liberal spirits of our day, as well as on all of those who crowd the "middle of the road," that the crusade for nontaxation and world disunity should invite even that fragment of idealistic devotion that rallies around the pages of the *National Review,* and that the young lady from the Bronx should remain as torn by indecision as she was that evening on Long Island.

CHAPTER 14

Challenge to the Beat

ONE GROWS OLDER, harshly reminded at a football game that the young men playing had not yet been born at the time of one's own commencement. There recurs the doubt as to whether anything strongly felt or believed extends across the line of generations, or whether it is the soliloquy of a lonesome left end.

I began with some informal remarks about the beat generation and there are those who may feel a certain dissatisfaction because I have not explored the matter in any depth. I hope I have made it clear, however, that I am concerned about older types, about those whom I would roughly call my own contemporaries, give or take ten years, who have achieved one of the varieties of "adjustment" to the condition of stability, a beatness not to be confused with beatitude.

In summer I live in Westport, Connecticut, and on the train to New York there is a moment shortly after 125th Street when we pass the slums of East Harlem. This is soon after a magazine's billboard ad preaching togetherness, and most of my trainmates are buried in the *Herald Tribune* or *The Wall Street Journal* or their emotional equivalents, wherein the proposition is affirmed that America has solved all its deep economic problems and must now deal only with the new complexities of general prosperity and the petty exasperations of life in suburbia, and so forth.

And on the steaming days when one sees from the train window multitudes of kids fighting for a place under the street shower, one thinks of the editors of *Fortune* grappling with the problem of crab grass, which is no trivial problem for any of us.

In that interval there is also the sense that I know what I care about, and that I am entirely alienated from those students of "status-seeking" who regard the view from the window of this train as alien and irrelevant to their conclusions about the amiable condition of American society. For they are talking about people who have made it, and still wish to make it on a bigger scale.

In an editor's life, especially if he is identified with what is known as a "crusading liberal newspaper," there are intermittent knocks on the door. One learns to steel one's self against the press agent and the proselytizing vegetarian. But one also becomes conscious of a vast array of people in trouble, ranging from those who are at war with a predatory, scheming landlord to those who have been the victims of the listless, lifeless procedure of our lower judicial system, and have been "defended" by court-appointed attorneys whose concern is often the prompt conclusion of the litigation so that they may return to their more profitable labors.

During the decade I have edited the *Post* it has rarely occurred to me that I had a shortage of causes, the common lament of some of the aging liberals and precocious juveniles of our time. I have been, on the contrary, oppressed by the sense that there was far more to be done in the simple interests of justice, fairness, decency, of even the smallest kindness, than our small staff could possibly hope to do.

It has become commonplace in the elder liberal set to dismiss such doings as a form of "ritualistic liberalism" quite unrelated to the larger aspects of our time. The squalor of our slums, the frustrations of the aged, the impoverishment of our hospitals, the desperate inadequacy of our school plant, the misery of migrant workers, the tortuous complexities created by automation, the pitiless pressures of status seeking in suburbia—all these, we are told, are "marginal" areas somehow remote from the mainstream of our national never-never land, where nearly everybody never had it so good.

It is not my desire to minimize the American achievement. I suggest only that we are in danger of convincing ourselves that nobody could ever have it better, and that the ease experienced by a one-time radical intellectual now employed by Mr. Ford's Fund for the Republic is the common denominator of American existence, equaled only by the inheritor of an industrial fortune.

Is it that all battles have been fought and won, or that many of those who used to care about the combat have wearied of the fray, and that a younger generation is uninspired by the shabby, colorless political symbols and slogans of our time?

As I was completing this book I was struck by a passage in a volume called *Conviction*, first published in Great Britain and reflecting the attitudes of those angry young and middle-aged men who have continued to participate in the political engagements of their time. I was especially intrigued by a passage in an essay called "The State of Stalemate" written by Norman Mackenzie:

Things are not so simple now. For years we have lacked causes —or should I say that for years we have been unable to recognize them? It does not matter which way you put it. Something happened to paralyze both passion and action. True, there were causes. To me, the peril of nuclear war seems just as great a threat as Hitler's form of genocide. I feel that some kind of agreement between East and West is just as urgent as collective security seemed in the thirties. I detest concepts of racial superiority. Much of Britain is still slum, still squalid, and even those parts of it that remain unspoiled are falling into the hands of the subtopians. I am appalled by the poverty that remains among the aged and the chronic sick, by the gross overcrowding of our State schools, by our overloaded and inadequate hospitals, our archaic prisons, blue laws and sexual attitudes that are a relic of pre-Freudian prejudice, by the triviality of our newspapers. I do not like a society in which the Establishment is riddled by snobbery and false values. And in all this I know that I am not alone, nor am I alone in saying this. But many who have complained most, like Sir Orlando Drought in Trollope's novel *The Prime Minister*, that "everything is dead" in politics, have somehow lacked the effort or will to liven everything up. They felt restless, perhaps, cynical more often; but too often they talked themselves into a mood of resignation and retreated into private worlds.

This does not say everything I should want to have said, but it expresses a mood with which I feel more closely identified than with much of the writing of American liberalism. What Mackenzie omitted in this passage (but at least tentatively suggested elsewhere) is that the simplicity of causes has also been brutally diminished by the Russian experience. The corruption of the egalitarian Marxist vision in the realities of Russian life—and in what has occurred in other areas of the Communist empire—has blurred the lines once so meaningful to those of us "old enough to remember and young enough to hope." There may be nothing quite as simple as the war in Spain seemed to be (until we read *Homage to Catalonia* by George Orwell), and there is nothing we could have done about the Hungarian rebellion as clear-cut as the formation of an international brigade, because it all ended too soon, and in any case, there was always the atomic bomb on the horizon.

Yet the fact remains that it is not a matter of whether there is anything left to be done, but whether the confusions and disappointments of the last two decades have destroyed our will and desire to do anything, and whether we have communicated—however indistinctly and falteringly—to those younger than ourselves the sense that our failure justifies their apathy.

I trust I have avoided suggesting a simplistic view of life in which the wisdom of politics can resolve all the sadness and mystery of existence. This I do not believe. I believe only that we can create the condition under which a maximum of human potentiality may be realized. Conflict is in the nature of the human beast, and I envisage no Utopia free of all strife; it might be rather a dull place if we found it.

It is not irrelevant that what purports to be in part a survey of the condition of American liberalism has virtually ignored the state of the Marxist fragments in our society. But I think that these sects have no serious relevance to this discussion except insofar as they stimulate a certain amount of self-appraisal.

Marxism taught us some things about economic behavior. But it taught us little about human behavior, and about the infinitely varied range of possibilities confronting us. Its barrenness was most sharply revealed with respect to the nature of life itself, its limitations, its pathos, its ultimate perplexity. It might almost be said that one had to abandon Marxism—whether in its Stalinist or Trotskyist or any other version—the moment one confronted the fact of death and a simultaneous awareness of the fleeting nature of any of our earthly triumphs.

With that awareness, now as two decades ago, one still has to choose between engagement and indifference, and to do so without self-righteousness about the choice. In my lifetime I have known a lot of men and women who preferred encounter to escape; I think at once of such varied figures as Roger Baldwin, Norman Thomas, Osmond Fraenkel (who happens to be my father-in-law), Dave Dubinsky, Walter Reuther, Sol Levitas, Reinhold Niebuhr, Elmer Davis.

It is embarrassing to mention any names because I know the omissions are so numerous, and because even the casual roster may be open to sectarian scrutiny. Nor do I suggest that each is a simple character dedicated to justice and freedom, and spared any of the torment of doubt and indecision visited on ordinary mortals. But by and large they have found life zestful and rewarding even when facing ambiguity and disappointment in the enterprises to which they have committed themselves.

Against them the cult of complexity and disavowal seems strangely uninspired. I also find those who have frankly abandoned hope preferable both to those who are sure they have got the system licked or are disdainful of those who are still fighting it.

This is however hardly an attempt to record an honor roll or produce a list of villains. It is only to say that, amid all the reversals and blandness of an age so peculiarly geared to complacency, I find a certain solace in the awareness that so many warm-blooded, serious men have had the time of their lives refusing to be beat.

I do not intend to seem content with all the old battle cries of liberalism, nor to dispute the need for variety and imagination in the presentation of the liberal case. I am aware that the discontents of which I have written are far more elusive and far less subject to simple political formulation than the general collapse of morale induced by the great breakdown of 1929. But is mass hunger and fiscal bankruptcy the only climate in which men can be persuaded to take a new look at their world? It is the contention of most of these pages that, in a certain sense, there is more rather than less to quarrel about in a society that has achieved some measure of affluence but finds itself steadily more insecure.

Perhaps the most cogent manifesto for a revived liberalism was contained in a memorandum written in 1959 by Arthur Schlesinger, Jr., entitled "The Shape of National Politics to Come."

He sees the lethargic era nearing an end and a new political ferment rising. "One feels that increasing numbers are waiting for a trumpet to sound," he writes. "The condition of national exhaustion is evidently coming to an end . . . In time, the collecting discontent will find a national voice (like Theodore Roosevelt in 1901 and Franklin Roosevelt in 1933). Then there will be a breakthrough into a new political epoch."

In the new age, Schlesinger contends, a resurgent liberalism will find itself more deeply involved with the concept of "the public interest" and "the national plant"—our "national investment in *people* (education, health, welfare, equal opportunity):"

If Democratic state organizations suppose that victory is inevitable in 1960, and that any political hack is going to win, regardless of his qualifications, then the party as a whole will very probably forfeit the opportunity which lies ahead. The American people are going to demand creative leadership, and they will not accept a collection of routine mediocrities with loud voices and stale phrases. The nation is at last coming out of the Eisenhower trance; it is belatedly awakening to the desperate need for new ideas, for intelligence, for innovation and vision in our public life. Unless the Democratic Party meets that need, it may have to watch an unsurpassed opportunity pass it by.

There is no guarantee, he warns, that the Democrats will inherit this political future. Indeed, it is hard to see how such a future can be born so long as both parties play the politics of stalemate. That is why I have earlier suggested that the most fruitful course for liberals in the Democratic Party is to abandon their concern for "party unity" and to recognize that only in disunity can ultimate strength be found. So long as men of instinctive decency feel compelled to remain on speaking terms with the Eastlands of the Democratic Party, they will be faithless to themselves and incapable of evoking idealism in others.

We are often told that Franklin D. Roosevelt set the style for liberal political men when he learned to live in peace with the right-wing Southern brethren. But that was a time when economic issues took precedence and when the quest for racial equality had not yet assumed its explosive force in America and other world areas. Moreover, it is tiresome to hear every act of modern political deceit defended as being in "the Roosevelt tradition." FDR was not infallible, and his memory is hardly served by awed reference to one of his less attractive traits.

Perhaps Schlesinger's estimate of an approaching political revival is premature. It may be we have not yet reached the point at which sufficient numbers of men are prepared for the risks and unpleasantnesses that confrontation of the duality within the parties requires. Nor would I venture a prophecy as to where the first breach will occur: certainly it is within the boundaries of possibility, as Schlesinger suggests, that Nelson Rockefeller can still eventually effect the kind of revolution within the Republican Party that Theodore Roosevelt engineered in another time. It seems equally clear that the political future of Hubert Humphrey rests on his ability and willingness to re-enact on an even larger scale the divisive civil rights uprising that he led at the Democratic Convention of 1948.

But this is not a campaign tract dedicated to any man's candidacy. I have been addressing myself to the drab listlessness that afflicts our political bodies; I have been urging that rejuvenated liberal leadership can light new fires.

My own sense of the general direction liberalism must pursue emerges, I hope, from these pages. Men may differ on priorities with respect to various matters; it is arguable whether at this stage we ought to be more concerned with the monotonous isolation under which so many labor or with the unfulfillment so many find in leisure. There are those who feel the disintegration of our educational plant demands treatment more urgently than our appalling disregard for the aged and the sick. There are those, including Schlesinger, who contend that it is the quality of American life—its schools, its cultural institutions, its "plant"—which must command more and more of our attention while others see the banishment of inequity and poverty as primary targets for today.

I do not seek to arbitrate among these conflicting claims; the enumeration of them suggests only how false it is to view the major business of democracy as done.

Clearly, however, there are top priorities: the quest for survival (without surrender), the assurance of equal rights for all Americans, the reaffirmation of the freedoms so battered during the dark age of McCarthy, the assertion of a generous American image that will give hope to the hungry and hounded of the world.

If it could be said of our time that we succeeded on the one hand in removing the specter of nuclear warfare and bringing full emancipation to 18,000,000 American Negroes, could it be said that this was a dull time, and that these goals were unworthy of large effort?

It is when one contemplates the diversity of the matters at hand that so many who aspire to political leadership appear so small and so dull. The Vogue's gallery of candidates includes many who are estimable, cautious, unprovocative, careful, adroit, calculating, unventurous, steeped in a passion for office that dwarfs and suppresses all other fervor, preoccupied with the tawdry deals and double talk and double cross that seem so often to have become the substance as well as the surface of our politics.

If the young seem beat and the old seem bored, let the movers and shakers look to themselves for the answer. Rarely has there been a time that clamored so loudly for valor and initiative, for the unconventional political act, the uninhibited word, the unequivocal thought spoken, in the Japanese phrase, "as if one were dead," and no longer prey to mortal pressure and vanity. Rarely have so many men acted in such a time as if the way to glory was through the glib evasion, the discreet retreat, the soft smile. But they may not have the last word.

INDEX

Walter, Francis, 45
Waring, Thomas, 141
Washington Post and Times Herald,
    100, 138
Wehrwein, Austin C., 26
Welch, Joseph, 180–183
Wells, H. G., 76
Weyl, Walter, 33
White, William S., 54
Williams, Tennessee, 156

Wilson, Charles E., 90, 93, 94
Wyatt, Wilson, 59

Yale University, 220
Yeats, William Butler, 176
Young Communist League, 168, 170,
    227
Young People's Socialist League, 15

Zwicker, Ralph W., 180

ABOUT THE AUTHOR

A native of New York City, where he was born in 1915, James A. Wechsler has been editor of the New York *Post* since 1949. His editorial career began at Columbia University, where he was editor of the Columbia *Spectator* from 1934 to 1935. The following year he was editor of *The Student Advocate*. In 1938 he became assistant editor of the *Nation* magazine, and in 1940 moved to the old *PM* newspaper as Labor editor. In 1942 he was made *PM*'s Washington Bureau Chief, serving in that capacity until 1944. He next served with the Anti-Cartel Division of the United States Military Government in Germany. In 1946 he joined the New York *Post* as Washington correspondent.

Mr. Wechsler is the author of *Revolt on the Campus, Labor Baron* and *The Age of Suspicion.* He is co-author, with Harold Lavine of *War Propaganda and the United States.*